THE WICCAN WAY

THE WICCAN WAY

SALLY MORNINGSTAR

WALKING STICK PRESS

Cincinnati, Ohio

First published in the U.K. in 2003 by Godsfield Press Ltd., Laurel House,
Station Approach, Alresford, Hampshire SO24 9JH, U.K.

www.godsfieldpress.com

2 4 6 8 10 9 7 5 3 1

Distributed to the trade markets in North America by
Walking Stick Press, an imprint of F&W Publications, Inc.
4700 East Galbraith Road, Cincinnati, OH 45236
Tel: 1-800-289-0963

Illustrator: Sarah Young. Page 10 P. Mills
Photographer: Mike Hemsley at Walter Gardiner
Additional photography: Sally Morningstar
Project Designer: Alison Hughes
Project Editor: Nicola Wright

Photographic Models: Genevieve Applebee, Christine Post,
Stephen Francis, Jozef Francis, Sarah Howerd, Laurie Morningstar

Designed and produced for Godsfield Press by The Bridgewater Book Company

Printed in China

ISBN 1-58297-269-9

Dedicated to my sister Jude
and the memory of my brother Jomps

Author Acknowledgments

*My thanks go to my editors and designers at the Bridgewater Book Company and Godsfield Press and to Angie Francesco for
all the beautiful gifts and healing she brings to this Earth. To Tu Shien, who remains a close friend despite (or is it because of?)
all my eccentricities! To Ruby Scrumptious for her waggable loyalty and writing companionship. My deepest gratitude goes
to Merlin and the most illustrious Verdhandi. Heartfelt wishes, too, to dearest L.J., all my hedgewitches, the dragons, the Shining
Ones, and the Ancestors. Thanks also to P. Mills for his contributions and to all people of planet Earth—may we
meet in peace and love in the Circle once more.*

The publisher would like to thank the following for the use of props:
Hand-crafted swords, athames, and ritual metalwork from Neil Hewitt at The Seven Swords of Wayland, Tel: 01458 447498;
Wiccan crafts and equipment from Tree Keeble at The Wicked Fairy; Wiccan tools from The Witchcraft Shop, Glastonbury;
sword from Stringtown Supplies: www.stringtownsupplies.co.uk, Tel: (01323) 488844; pentacle platter and candlesticks from
The Green Man— www.greenmanbooks.co.uk, E-mail greenmangallery@lineone.net.

For details of Sally Morningstar's books, courses, and workshops, please visit www.sallymorningstar.com
or write to P.O. Box 2633, Radstock, Somerset BA3 5XR, U.K.
Information about local covens, magical supplies, crafts, moots (get-togethers),
and other pagan activities is available on the following websites:
thewickedfairy@hotmail.com
www.witchvox.com
www.paganfederation.org
www.Museumofwitchcraft.com
www.witchcraftshop.co.uk
www.newmoonoccultshop.co.uk
www.thebluemoon.co.uk

CONTENTS

PREFACE

This book provides a beautifully simple introduction to Wicca as a spiritual practice that gives you lots of step-by-step advice and guidance on the Craft. It will help give you a clear understanding of how to live your life following the Wiccan principles of honoring the Earth, the natural world, yourself, and others.

Wicca is an ancient nature/fertility religion. In our deep historical past, respecting nature was necessary for survival. Communities thrived or died based on the availability of food, water, and shelter. The continuation of life depended on the ability to hunt and grow food. With this in mind, it is easy to understand the reasons that people since ancient times have venerated the natural world. Nature was like a Mother to our ancestors because she provided for all of their needs. The four Greater *Sabbats* (Wiccan agricultural festivals) of Imbolc, Beltaine, Lughnasadh, and Samhain were established to help the Mother to turn the wheel of Creation and thus enact the continuation of life on Earth.

Today that wheel is being compromised because modern society often disregards the natural world. Wicca helps us to work cooperatively with nature and with the forces of Creation so that we can live in peace, joy, and harmony with each other. With Wicca we are connected to our rightful place on the Earth as guardians of the planet, not abusers and violators of her.

The Wiccan Way explains many Wiccan practices and beliefs, including the background to the Craft, the magical tools, the arrangement of a Wiccan altar, and how to perform rituals and ceremonies. Guidelines are also given that will help you develop yourself spiritually so that you can embody the powers of nature within your own being. Many people assume that Wicca is simply spells, bells, and charm bags. It is far more profound than this, for it can provide the link between our essence and the essence of Creation. In Wicca we believe that the Goddess is the Creator, supported, protected, and served by her consort the Horned God. When we honor the natural world and the powers of Creation in a rightful way, we are given the most wondrous gift from the Mother Goddess: her magic. This magic is beyond mortal words. It is the space between, the moment beyond, the dream come true. It opens our eyes to the most glorious truth and evolves our spirit to the point that it is free and happy and at peace.

That magic is only a moment away. If we only had the eyes to see it and the heart to feel it, we would be aware that it is around us and within us all the time. *The Wiccan Way* aims to help you to find the magical dimension, that natural way of being that brings such joy to the spirit, so that at last you can discover the magic of who you really are and celebrate that unique journey back to yourself.

The Wiccan Way also gives guidance on the practical applications of the Craft with regard to daily life, offering details on healing, psychic protection, rites of passage, and finding your magical name. It explains spell crafting and making your own ritual equipment, but most important of all, it takes you on the journey back to your spirit, to your heart, and to your innocence. I hope you enjoy reading *The Wiccan Way*. May it reveal your own beauty to you and show you the way home.

Sally Morningstar

DEFINITION OF COMMON WICCAN TERMS

ATHAME	*a witch's sacred dagger*
BOOK OF SHADOWS	*a witch's sacred book*
COVEN	*a group of Wiccans under the guidance of a High Priestess*
DEVA	*a flower spirit*
DRYAD	*a tree spirit*
ESBAT	*a coven meeting less formal than a Sabbat*
GAIA	*Ancient Greek Earth Goddess*
GNOMES	*Elemental spirits of the Earth Element*
HORNED GOD	*the primary male deity of witchcraft*
LEMNASCATE	*a symbol of eternity, drawn like a figure of eight*
LIBATION	*a fluid offering made to a deity*
MOTE	*"may" or "shall" ("So mote it be!" = "May it be so!" or "So shall it be!")*
PSYCHISM	*psychic ability and perception*
SACRED CIRCLE	*a sacred area in which formal ritual working is to be performed*
SAGE SMUDGE STICK	*bundled herbal stick of sage leaves*
SAMHAIN	*(pronounced "sow-en") the festival of remembering the ancestors, marking the end of the Celtic year and the dawning of the new year, and honoring the last of the current year's harvest festivals*
SYLPHS	*Elemental Spirits of the Air Element*
UNDINES	*Elemental Spirits of the Water Element*

WHAT IT MEANS TO BE WICCAN

Blessed Be!

o be Wiccan is to venerate the Goddess and her consort the Horned God, and to follow the ethics and practices of the Old Religion. This ancient pagan tradition existed long before the establishment of the Church.

Wicca honors the Earth as our spiritual Mother (the Goddess) and the Sky and the wildness of nature as our spiritual Father (the Horned God). In practice this means that we venerate nature and the planet upon which we live. We endeavor not to harm anyone or anything, because to us these are all our brothers and sisters with an equal right to exist. Wicca is a tradition that works to harm none in thought, word, or deed. Anyone, therefore, who says they are a witch but works otherwise should not be considered an authentic practitioner.

Witchcraft is still the only spiritual tradition that raises the female above the male, in contrast to patriarchal religions such as Christianity and Judaism. They venerate an almighty male deity, with little positive mention of the female at all. Because of its veneration of a Goddess, Wicca follows the moral values associated with feminine spiritual powers—such as love, peace, and joy—rather than the more masculine religious attitudes of domination, control, and fear.

Witches work by peaceful means, seeking to unite rather than to divide, to be of service to our communities, and to be the healers, counselors, and the guardians of all life on this Earth. This is because we see ourselves as the children of the Goddess and the Horned God that we venerate. When this is a truth within us, we can only ever love and look after what they have so lovingly created for us.

A BRIEF HISTORY OF WICCA

The term *Wicca* originates from the Anglo-Saxon word *wicce* (pronounced "witcha"), the basis for the current pronunciation of our modern word *witch*. It was repopularized as a term to describe witchcraft in the 1950s by the late Gerald Gardner. Along with his High Priestess, the late Doreen Valiente, he established Gardnerian witchcraft.

Witchcraft has a stormy past. It has been an object of much malice and hostility, largely based upon hysteria and fabrication. Calling someone a witch was at one time enough to condemn them, so that term quickly became a way to brand absolutely any passing innocent as evil. What was overlooked was the fact that at no point has there been a devil in Wicca, much less any concept of evil or sin. Satan is, in fact, a Christian demon. Yet because of the hundreds of years of propaganda against witchcraft, people, even today, have a primal fear about it being evil and will indiscriminately blame it for all sorts of ills.

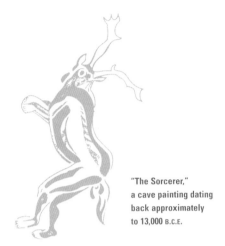

"The Sorcerer," a cave painting dating back approximately to 13,000 B.C.E.

Witches, pagans, and heathens have all been treated as *heretics* (a term used to define those whose views opposed the Church) throughout the centuries. It is difficult, therefore, to write a definitive history of witchcraft and because of persecution, much of this important history has been lost or destroyed. However, we know that there was veneration of the feminine form 27,000 years ago because our prehistoric ancestors carved female fertility figurines called the Venuses. Going back 15,000 years, cave paintings also reveal that the people in our past connected magically with animals and the powers of nature.

Witchcraft existed peacefully in various guises for thousands of years. It was not until metal was discovered and forged into the sword that a great deal of bloody and aggressive cultural upheaval began across the globe with battles, conquests, and invasions. Warrior gods were venerated, and it did not take long before one vengeful almighty male God (Jehovah or Yahweh) was created to

The "Venus" of Willendorf dated around 25,000 B.C.E.

reflect the beliefs of this warrior class. Many innocents have suffered throughout the ages because of religion. Members of the peasant classes of the Middle Ages (who were the midwives, doctors, counselors, and healers of the time) were singled out for discrimination whether they were actually witches or not.

Witchcraft itself went underground in order to survive, and emerged again in Europe only in the 1950s after the repeal of the Witchcraft Act. This means that it has been within only the last fifty years that witches have legally been able to announce their presence again. Today, Wicca has many varied practices, including Traditional, Gardnerian, Alexandrian, Celtic, Faery, Dianic, Solitary, and Hereditary. Although they provide different flavors, all varieties venerate the feminine above the masculine. They also all honor the Wiccan rule to "harm none" and to work for the highest good to the best of their ability.

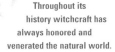

Throughout its history witchcraft has always honored and venerated the natural world.

WICCAN FAITH AND BELIEF

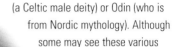

W iccan faith and belief is focused on the Goddess and the Horned God, the two primary deities of witchcraft. They are sometimes referred to as the Mother Goddess and Father God or "the Mighty Ones."

These two deities have many subdivisions, with archetypes for every conceivable need from sea travel to childbirth. Their influences have no boundaries, and have been especially strong in Ancient Egypt, Greece, Rome, Northern Europe, India, and the Middle East. This explains why certain witches work with Isis while others worship Hecate and still others choose Cernunnos

(a Celtic male deity) or Odin (who is from Nordic mythology). Although some may see these various forms as being different, they are all aspects of the primary Goddess and God that all witches venerate.

Wicca is a tradition of respect and tolerance. This is translated in the *Wiccan Rede* (credo):

> *Bide the Wiccan law ye must,*
> *in perfect love and perfect trust.*
> *Eight words the Wiccan rede fulfill;*
> *an it harm none, do what ye will.*
> *What ye send forth comes back to thee, so ever*
> *mind the law of three.*
> *Follow this with mind and heart. Merry ye meet*
> *and merry ye part.*

If you wish to live your life according to Wiccan values, it is important that you achieve a deep understanding of what the Wiccan Rede means. "Perfect love and perfect trust" refers to our original state of innocence in which our hearts are open and our feelings are receptive to Divine will. The principle of harming none excludes us from, for example, gossiping, back-biting, negative thinking, and hurting another's feelings intentionally. Living this way requires great integrity.

HONORING THE GODDESS
AND THE HORNED GOD

Wiccans honor the Goddess and Horned God by working to embody the essence or spirit of these deities within their own being. This means that the goal of the female witch is to personify the Goddess, while the male endeavors to incorporate the qualities of the Horned God into his daily life.

In contrast to some other religions which teach about an afterlife where people will be rewarded in heaven or punished in hell, Wicca brings spirituality firmly into the present moment. In Wicca there is no separation between the physical and the spiritual.

In Wicca, there is no sin in the flesh. As long as we harm none and live with rightful awareness of our Oath, we see our bodies as being part of our human nature. This means that we celebrate our lives in a spirit of gratitude for the gifts that we have, including our bodies. Very often, people preparing for initiation into the Craft must first release personal inhibitions, shame, and guilt. These forms of social conditioning can be barriers to entering the Wiccan way with confidence. This step is not taken because we practice deviant activities. Instead, it represents a liberation of the spirit within the flesh. As a result, we are proud to be who we are and proud to go naked if needs be, regardless of shape, size, or wrinkles!

To honor the Goddess and Horned God, Wiccans must therefore become unashamed of themselves. This is the first step to understanding the profundity of truly being able to embody and honor the Sacred.

MEETING THE GODDESS AND HORNED GOD

Wiccans recognize the Goddess and Horned God as being part of each of us, as well as being everywhere around us. We can meet them whenever we wish. As our spiritual Mother and Father, they will always give us guidance and love. In Wicca, they are Mother Earth and Father Sky.

The purpose of meeting with the Goddess and Horned God is to develop and build an intimate relationship with them as if they are loved family members, and to realize that as their children we are always able to turn to them for spiritual comfort and support. Meeting them helps us to realize that we are never alone.

The Goddess and Horned God are always with those who honor them; it is we who often ignore their presence. View the Earth as the body of the Goddess, and the sky and wildness of nature as the domain of the Horned God.

❶ Prepare a room (or, in summer, find a quiet place outdoors that attracts you).

❷ Calm the inner self by breathing in to a slow count of four, pausing for a count of four, breathing out for a count of four, and pausing for a count of four. This is called the Fourfold Breath (see page 49). Continue until you feel centered.

❸ Let your spirit flow with love over the Earth and then down into her through your feet. Draw her essence back up into your being through your feet, just as tree roots would.

❹ Now, raise your arms toward the sky in a "V" shape, palms facing inward, and let your spirit flow into the skies, the breeze, and the sun. When you feel connected, slowly bring your arms down in front of you to waist height, a little out to your sides. Give your love to the trees, creatures, plants, and flowers. Then with palms facing upward before you, imagine the love of the Horned God flowing toward you and filling your spirit with his love.

TAKING A MAGICAL OATH

A Magical Oath is your solemn promise to honor Wiccan values and is made to the Goddess and Horned God. Wiccans frequently call the Goddess and Horned God "The Mighty Ones." The Oath is made to them through you, and so you are making this promise to your higher self as well as to them.

The reason for taking the Oath is twofold:
i to ensure that you are prepared to follow the Wiccan guidelines of harming none, and
ii to raise yourself to your highest potential in thought, word, and deed from that day on.
The Magical Oath also affirms that you will not use the Craft in selfish ways.

❶ Create a magical atmosphere around your altar (see pages 22–23) with candles, incense, and greenery (as well as appropriate music if you like). Choose a special time, such as midnight or dawn.

❷ Prepare yourself by bathing and then anointing yourself with sacred oil blended by putting five drops of frankincense into two teaspoons (10 ml) of carrier oil. Using your finger, anoint above your pubic bone, as well as your feet, palms, breasts, heart, throat, and forehead.

❸ Light your candles and stand facing the altar. Ring a bell to start. Then visualize the Goddess and Horned God standing before you witnessing your Oath.

❹ Place one hand on your heart and the other before you, palm forward, and say the following:

"I do solemnly swear in the presence of you Mighty Ones to honor the ancient way, to love the Earth, and respect all life. I pledge from this day on to work only for the highest good; to strive to harm none in thought, word, or deed; and to extend myself beyond my human limitations to unite with You as my true Self. I now welcome the sacred ways into my Spirit. By your grace, the veil shall be lifted and I shall be deemed worthy of your love."
Bow your head and say, *"My Lady, my Lord, witness this my solemn Oath."*

Ring a bell to close.

GETTING STARTED WITH WICCA

*"And round and round the circle spun
Until the gates swung wide ajar that bar the boundary of the Earth
From fairy realms that shine afar."*

THE WITCHES' BALLAD, DOREEN VALIENTE

To begin Wiccan practice we need to find Goddess and Horned God figurines, which don't have to be expensive. We also need to obtain our four Wiccan altar tools: the athame (a witch's sacred dagger, used only in rituals), the wand, the chalice, and the pentagram, which represent the four Elements of Air, Fire, Water, and Earth respectively. Wiccans lay out these tools on their altar during all ritual and ceremonial work because they represent the four Elemental quarters of East, South, West, and North in the Circles that we cast. More details about the Elemental tools can be found on page 18.

We will also need to consider where we will cast our working Circle, whether indoors or out. For an altar, you can use any simple object, such as a small table, a chest or box, or a natural one, such as a tree stump or stone. Primary factors to consider are privacy, warmth, comfort, and personal safety. Many Wiccan rituals are performed during the witching hour, which is around midnight. That is because all Wiccan practices aim to take the spirit beyond the activities of mundane daily life into dimensions that are less frequently realized, such as dawn, dusk, and midnight. However, this does not preclude you from performing rituals at any time of the day or night.

This chapter reveals how and when to cleanse, bless, and consecrate items and areas prior to any magical work. Attention should be given to our magical equipment, robes, physical body, and any special jewelry we may wear during rituals. Casting a working Circle creates a place beyond ordinary space and time where magic happens and the cares of the world can be left behind.

WICCAN TOOLS

The most significant tools are the athame for Air, the wand for Fire, the chalice for Water, and the pentagram for Earth. Wiccans also require candles and candle-holders, icons of the Goddess and Horned God, and two small containers for salt and spring water, plus a Book of Shadows. All of a witch's personal tools should have meaning. It is preferable to have a simple chalice received with love from a friend than a crystal chalice encrusted with jewels that you have bought for the purpose of being impressive.

Athame

The athame is the witch's sacred dagger that traditionally has a black handle and a double-edged metal blade. It is important that this knife is not used for any purpose other than ritual work. A knife from your kitchen can become an athame as long as it is used only in rituals after its consecration.

Wand

The wand is a piece of wood up to about 18 inches (46 cm) long that is hand-picked from a live tree. This must be done respectfully and with awareness. Some Wiccans have elaborate wands with crystals, feathers, and magical inscriptions. It is a personal choice whether yours is plain or decorated, although traditionally wands are usually plain.

Chalice

The chalice is a cup or grail normally filled with mead, cider, wine, or apple juice. It can be highly elaborate or delicate, or simply a wine glass that has been consecrated and then kept only for magical work.

Pentagram

The pentagram is a circular piece of wood or metal with the five-pointed star either etched or painted within a circle upon it. It is normally placed in the center of the altar between the two candles.

Book of Shadows

The Book of Shadows is the witch's personal sacred book in which rituals, spells, charms, and documents are stored and referred to during magical work.

Staff

Many witches have a personal staff. Some choose simple straight staffs, others have shaped ones, and yet others prefer the "Y"-shaped forked stang that represents the Horned God.

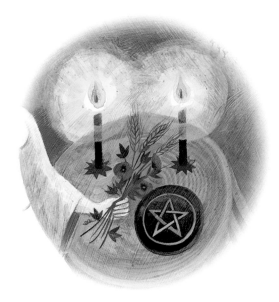

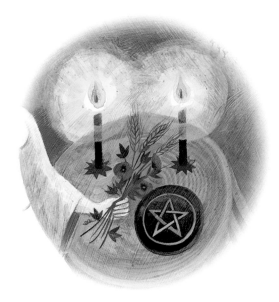

Consecrating magical tools and equipment

Any items that you use for magical work should be cleansed, blessed, sanctified, and activated for the highest good before use.

❶ Lay out your altar (see pages 22–23) with your statuette icons of the Goddess and Horned God and four representations of the Elements as listed below:

- a small bowl of salt for Earth in the North
- an incense stick for Air in the East
- a red candle for Fire in the South
- a small bowl of spring water for Water in the West.

❷ Lay the items to be consecrated in the center, over your pentagram if you wish. Light the incense and the candle and sit quietly for a few moments.

❸ Take up an item and pass it through the incense smoke and say, "*By the powers of Air, may this* [name the item] *now be cleansed, blessed, and sanctified for the highest good.*" Pass it across the candle flame a few times and say, "*By the powers of Fire, may this* [name the item] *now be cleansed, blessed, and sanctified for the highest good.*" Now sprinkle it with a little water and say, "*By the powers of Water may this* [name the item] *now be cleansed, blessed, and sanctified for the highest good.*" Finally sprinkle it with a little salt and say, "*By the powers of Earth may this* [name the item] *now be cleansed, blessed, and sanctified for the highest good.*"

❹ Hold your item in both hands, face North, and say, "*By the powers of the Goddess and the Great Horned God, may this* [name the item] *now be blessed and sanctified for the highest good of all. So mote it be!*" (this means "So shall it be!")

GETTING STARTED WITH WICCA

19

CREATING SACRED SPACE

 n Wicca, all of Creation is sacred. To us, the world is like a beautiful garden that was created by our Mother and Father for us—their children. In creating sacred space, we allow ourselves the time to feel the sacredness that is always present.

All environments, however, can be affected by pollutants (whether these are chemical or emotional in nature). Therefore, the first step to creating sacred space is to cleanse the area. The next steps are to bless and invoke the sacred by visualizing light and love. Finally, we seal the area with some kind of protection.

Wiccans create sacred space prior to all magical working, before setting up a magical circle, and when an environment seems to need cleansing due to daily stresses and strains. You can create sacred space anywhere and at any time in order to lift atmospheres or in preparation for your magical activities.

❶ Cleansing Put three drops of Rose Geranium oil into a bowl of warmed spring water. Wash your hands, feet, and face with it before you start. This will ensure that your energy is psychically cleansed. Enter the environment you have chosen (it can be indoors or outdoors) and face North. Light a sage smudge stick and hold it before you, letting the smoke billow in that direction. Visualize all pollutants leaving with the smoke. Turn East and do the same, but this time imagine that all cruel words and deeds are departing. Turn South and visualize all stale, old, and tired energy being removed. Finally, turn West and visualize all pain and suffering being lifted.

Turn North to complete your circle. Bury the lit end of your smudge stick in a bowl of earth to douse it.

❷ Blessing Remain facing North and turn your palms toward it. Say the following blessing: *"And it be for highest good, may good now enter here and here remain."*

❸ Invoking Stretch your right arm up toward the sky and extend your left arm down toward the earth. Concentrating upon your left arm, call to Mother Goddess as follows: *"O Sweet Mother, giver of Grace, I ask that you bless this place with your loving heart and hold it in your wise embrace. So mote it be!"*

Focusing on your right arm, call to Father God as follows: *"Oh mighty One, Lord of all Nature and guardian of this Sacred Earth, I ask that you shield and secure this place with your protection. So mote it be!"*

Imagine the energy of a beautiful Mother rising through your arm and up to the heavens and the energy of a strong and reliable Father descending through your other arm down into the Earth. Stay in the experience for a few moments.

❹ Sealing Bring both arms to your heart and breathe with peace in your heart. Using the hand that you write with, draw a figure of eight (the symbol of eternity, called a lemnascate) from North to center in front of you, East to center, and so on until all four directions are completed.

ARRANGING A WICCAN ALTAR

An altar is used in many spiritual traditions. In Wicca, the ritual altar provides a focus for spiritual energy and is a place to put magical equipment during rituals and ceremonies. The Wiccan ritual altar is where we place the elemental tools, candles, and other equipment that we may require during a ritual or magical event, so that we do not have to leave the sacred circle once it is cast. This ritual altar is erected just before casting the circle and is dismantled after completion. You can, however, display your magical tools on other altars around your home if you wish, or store them away.

Your Wiccan ritual altar should be set up just before your magical event. It can include an altar cloth, although this is not compulsory. Your altar should be large enough to contain your equipment. A small, portable table or chest would be ideal. It is usually placed in the North, East, or center of the circle, depending upon your preference and practicality.

❶ Cover your table with an altar cloth if desired, and set the two candles on either side at the back. Many Wiccans use black candles; in Wicca, black is the color of peace, tranquillity, deep spirituality, and meditation. Consider your ritual to determine which color of candles best suits your focus or intent (see pages 50–51). Place your pentagram plate in the center of the table. The chalice— which is filled with apple juice, red wine, or cider—is then placed on the platter.

❷ Place small icons of the Goddess and Horned God on either side of the pentagram; and your athame (a witch's sacred dagger, used only in rituals) at the side. Place your wand on the other side of the pentagram. (See "Wiccan Tools," pages 18–19.) Position a small container of spring water and a small bowl of salt on either side of your pentagram plate. A saucer should be nearby for your libations. (A libation is a fluid offering made to the Goddess and Horned God from the chalice after the circle is cast but before you begin your actual ritual. First you pour your offering to the Goddess and then to the Horned God, after which you take a sip yourself.)

❸ Arrange any other ritual items (such as your bell, incense burner, and Book of Shadows) where there is space. Any other decorative items that in some way reflect your ritual or magical intent can also be included (such as fallen leaves in fall, a small Yule log in winter, bulbs in a small pot in spring, or a brightly-painted Sun icon in summer).

❹ When the altar is set up, light the candles and incense, and sound the bell. Then kneel for a few moments in meditation before it, consecrating it in your mind to the four Elemental guardians and dedicating it to the highest good, which is always under the guidance and protection of the Goddess and Horned God. You are now ready to begin your magical work. Ring the bell, extinguish the candles, and leave the area in preparation for entering again to start your ritual event or celebration.

A formal Wiccan altar,
displaying sacred tools
and equipment ready for
ritual work.

CASTING A SACRED CIRCLE

I n Wicca, a sacred circle is used to define the special area in which formal ritual working is to be performed. The circle is not a barrier; it is a doorway to another world, a magical and mystical place where the conditions and rules are different from the everyday world. The circle is also a container for your magical energy and any magical power that is raised, preventing it from dissipating until it is used. The Wiccan circle does not need to be drawn or marked on the ground; it is a spiritual energy that is visualized in the mind.

You can cast a sacred circle for all magical acts. Its size should comfortably contain those using it. You will need to perform certain actions and speak certain words aloud in a clear voice. A Wiccan altar should be placed in the north, center, or east of the circle.

❶ Prepare yourself by bathing, and clear and cleanse your chosen area. Set up your altar.

❷ Light your altar candles. Take your athame or sword from the altar and walk around your circle, saying: "*With this sacred blade I cast the circle of our craft. May it be a doorway to that sacred circle that is beyond space and time. Let it be a meeting place for all good, and may it repel all wickedness.*"

❸ Stand before your altar, pick up your bell, and say: "*In the names of the Goddess and the great Horned God, I cast this my/our working circle.*" Ring your bell.

❹ Return to the North, raise your blade high before you, and call out: "*Bear witness, Spirits of the North, ye guardians of Wicca.*" Go to the East, South, and West, and repeat appropriately.

❺ At the altar, put your salt bowl on the pentagram and lower the point of your athame into the bowl of salt, saying: "*I exorcise thee, oh creature of salt, that thou be purified and thus may aid me well.*" Put your water on the pentagram and take a pinch of salt and sprinkle it into the bowl of water. Lower the point of your athame into the water, saying: "*I cleanse and consecrate thee, Water of Life, that thou mayest bless this circle. In the names of the Goddess and Horned God, so mote it be!*"

❻ Take up the consecrated water and go slowly round the circle again (still clockwise), sprinkling a few drops along the line of the Circle, saying: "*I consecrate this sacred circle by the powers of Earth, Air, Fire, and Water. May the Goddess bestow her love herein, and the Horned God his honor.*" Take up your chalice, pour a small amount in the saucer for the Goddess and Horned God (libation), and then take a sip yourself. After this is completed, place the chalice behind or back on your pentagram.

Your circle is now cast and you can perform your specific activity here, such as a Sabbat ritual, making a charm, or healing. Complete your chosen focus and then move on to closing your circle.

Closing the circle

❶ Go to the North, hold up your blade, and say, "*Guardians and spirits of the* [North] *wind, this ritual is now done. I/We bid you hail and farewell. Hail and farewell.*" Repeat counterclockwise from North to West, to South, to East, and back to the North again.

❷ Extinguish your altar candles and bow your head at the altar, saying, "*I declare this sacred circle closed. So mote it be.*" Ring a bell to complete the closing and step out.

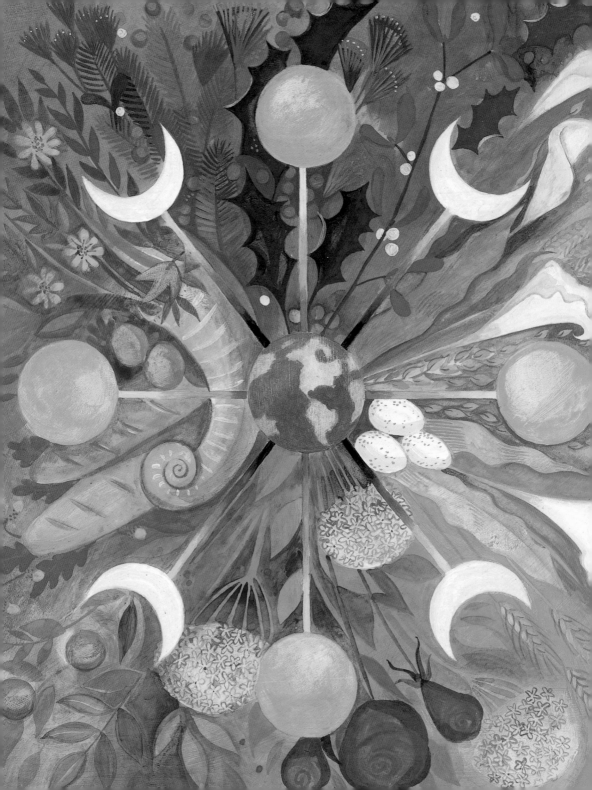

THE WICCAN CALENDAR

"Hoof and horn, hoof and horn, all that dies shall be reborn
Corn and grain, corn and grain, all that falls shall rise again."

TRADITIONAL WICCAN CHANT, IAN CORRIGAN

he Wiccan calendar is also referred to as the Wiccan Wheel of the Year. This wheel represents a full cycle of the seasons of spring, summer, fall, and winter. Each season brings certain gifts. In spring, it is new life, youth, potential, and the stirring of the seeds. In summer, it is warmth, light, and the vibrancy of nature growing. In fall, it is the harvest and the fruits of our labors. In winter, it is rest, introspection, and renewal. Each season is marked by a series of festivals to honor the particular qualities of each time of year. Wiccans help to turn the wheel of the seasons through both acknowledgment and by enactment of each seasonal focus through their rituals.

The Wiccan calendar includes four Greater Sabbats and four Lesser Sabbats. The four Greater Sabbats of Imbolc, Beltaine, Lughnasadh, and Samhain are also called the four agricultural festivals and are very ancient pagan rites. The four Lesser Sabbats are the spring (Ostara) and fall (Mabon) equinoxes and the winter (Yule) and summer (Litha) solstices, which are later additions to the Wiccan calendar. These Lesser Sabbats acknowledge distinctions between the forces of dark and light throughout the year, and fires or light are often significant.

By enacting what should occur as each season rises and falls, Wiccans empathically connect with the powers of Creation and effectively try to mirror what is happening in nature. For example, at Imbolc when the maiden Goddess returns to herald the birth of spring, Wiccans may actually invite a coven member dressed as a maiden in a veil and white robes into their homes. This way they literally welcome in the Spring.

INTRODUCTION TO THE FESTIVALS

The Greater Sabbats are highly spiritual occasions, undertaken with greatest regard and dignity. In all Wiccan rituals and ceremonies the sanctity and sacredness of the occasion is always honored and respected. Because these rituals are meant to embody the powers of Creation, they should be considered to be "serious" occasions. This does not mean that laughter, celebration, and joy are not present. These aspects are most often invited after the cakes and ale are introduced at the end of the ceremony. Sometimes there is a direction written specifically into the ritual event to, for example, dance and sing. Understanding the meaning of each festival allows Wiccans to write their own rituals that incorporate the flavor of each festival within their words.

THE GREATER SABBATS

Samhain. Colors—orange, black, white
Samhain (pronounced "sow-en") begins on the eve of November 1 (October 31) and marks the end of the Celtic year. Because this night is neither old nor new it stands at the threshold between. It is, therefore, associated with the ancestors and the otherworld. Samhain is the time when Wiccans honor the ancestors and perform divination.

Imbolc. Colors—white, pastels
Imbolc (pronounced "imolk") begins on the eve of February 2 (February 1) and marks the first spring fertility festival with the return of the maiden Goddess to the Earth as she brings in the dawning of spring. Wiccans make candlelit processions to sacred wells and springs, cleanse and bless local waterways, and invite the maiden (Spring) into their homes.

A shrine to the Earth Goddess, forming part of a public ritual performed at the Glastonbury Goddess Conference in 2002 by the Magpie Hedgewitches.

Beltaine. Colors—green, gold, red, white

Beltaine (pronounced "beall-te-nye") begins on the eve of May (April 30) and is one of the most magical of Wiccan festivals. It is the third fertility festival on the Wheel. It is associated with fairies, magic, and love. Anything magical and romantic is welcomed. Many couples get handfasted (married) at this festival. (Those ending a relationship may perform a hand-parting at this time.)

Lughnasadh. Colors—orange, ochre, brown

Lughnasadh (pronounced "loo-nah-sah") begins on the eve of August 1 (July 31) and is the first of the three Wiccan harvest festivals. It is in honor of the declining powers of the solar warrior god Lugh and gives thanks for the harvest about to be gathered. It is also a time to make an appeal for good weather until the crops are safely home. Traditionally bread is made and mead is brought to make an offering to the Goddess and Horned God that symbolizes our thanks for their bounty.

THE LESSER SABBATS

The four solar festivals or Lesser Sabbats occur at Yule around December 21 (the winter solstice), Ostara (around the spring equinox that falls on or around March 21), Litha around June 21 (the summer solstice), and Mabon around September 21 (fall equinox). Being fire or solar festivals, all light is usually extinguished before new fires or beacons are lit to mark the turning of the Wheel.

Yule altar—evergreens, vanilla, pine, cypress, mistletoe; red and gold.

Ostara altar—white cone lilies, seeds, grains, eggs; white and green.

Litha altar—the staff, roses, elderflower, meadowsweet, vervain; red and green.

Mabon altar—cornucopia, green man, stag, cider, acorns, bread; rich fall colors in all hues.

Votive altars to the Mighty Ones can be elaborate or simple. This simple Horned God altar, brightly colored and decked with ivy and lanterns, could sit above a fireplace.

WORKING WITH THE WHEEL OF THE YEAR

Since the Wheel of the Year symbolizes the turning of the seasons, you can have seasonal altars and plan seasonal activities and rituals that complement each time of year. Choose a place in your home that you can adjust as each season changes. For example, you can collect feathers, stones, mosses, leaves, flowers, and fruits to arrange on your seasonal altar. This helps you to make a deeper connection to the turning of the year.

It can be very helpful to keep a journal to record observations about your journey through the year. Linking with the natural world in this personal way will heighten your observances of when, for example, the first snowdrops appear or the hawthorn blossoms emerge. You can note bird migrations, flight patterns, dawn choruses, and anything else you like. You can walk through the twilight and perhaps meet with a badger on country lanes or receive a blessing from a swooping bat. Keeping records in a journal helps you connect to Nature. You begin to know when to expect certain things and at what time of day, night, or year they are most active. This way you will know roughly when you could gather meadowsweet or elderflowers, crab apples, or acorns, for example. It is very helpful to develop your own guide for which season you should gather your herbs, fruits, or nuts for magical work. It is always best to make your lotions, oils, or concoctions during the season when your ingredients are active. A holly essence, for example, is best made around Yule time, whereas rose petal water is best made in the warmer months.

"Man's Hand in Nature"—a sculpture by Lee Dickenson at the Royal Botanical Gardens, Bath, United Kingdom.

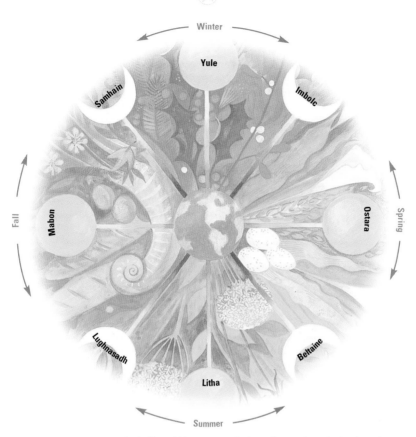

Experience what each season feels like within your own being. As the winter approaches, most of us begin to withdraw from social activity. With the promise of light, in contrast, we emerge and become much more active. This is a very simple example of how the seasons can affect us. More profound experiences can be had by standing at midnight on frosted grass during winter solstice, performing a magical salutation to the sun at dawn, or gathering the dew on Beltaine morn—said to be the gift of true love's nectar from the fairy King and Queen.

Build your confidence in performing the Greater Sabbat rituals that honor each season and then reach out to find your own ways of expressing each time of year, through ritual, poetry, storytelling, Craft working, or perhaps singing and drumming.

The great joy of Wicca is that it celebrates as well as venerates the natural world. Human beings are part of nature and so any way that we, the children of the Earth, wish to honor our spiritual Mother and Father is seen as an act of love toward them, as long as we remain sincere about it. Be confident in yourself and know there is no such thing as a mistake in Wicca when we are doing our best to act from the perspectives of love and respect. Experiment, explore, enjoy, and emulate these Wiccan ideals and, by the Grace of the Goddess, you will be shown her magic.

RHYTHMS OF THE MOON

CHAPTER THREE

The moon is intimately associated with the Triple Goddess of Maiden (new), Mother (full), and Crone (waning/dark). She holds deep occult secrets and is the revealer, the reflector, the inner guide. The moon is associated with magic, healing, fertility, conception, nature, water, women, dreams, psychism, and the weather. Her day of the week is Monday and her most potent power time is at full moon.

Lunar timing plays an integral part in magical work, because Wiccans believe that each weekday, each hour, each season, and each time of day has a distinct flavor to it which can be incorporated into the fabric of any magical work.

Each phase of the moon carries certain powers. New to full is for attraction, the actual full moon is for manifestation of desires and wishes, and the waning to dark is for release. To call for a new beginning, choose a waxing moon. For endings, release, or removal, choose a waning moon.

By referring to the chart opposite, you can make your own lunar charm bags, spells, and healing amulets simply by combining ingredients.

The new moon is associated with Artemis and Thoth and assists with conception of a variety of ideas, plans, and projects, including pregnancy. It can help other things in your life to grow as well. Seek the new moon to attract things to you.

The full moon, associated with Isis, Diana, Aradia, and Arianrhod, is powerful and should be approached with respect and reverence. Seek the full moon when you wish to manifest something in your life on a physical or practical level, such as a child.

The waning moon is ruled by Hecate, Cybele, and Cerridwen. It is the time when things can be cast away and released. It is also the time for banishings. The waning moon allows us to withdraw and to move inward. Time is given for reflection and release of that which is as yet unmanifested.

The dark moon is the one night when no moon is seen in the sky. Like the waning moon, it is governed by the dark goddesses who are also referred to as the wisdom keepers. It is, therefore, the best time to focus your efforts upon meditation. Insights can be gained by contemplation of your inner world. Chaos can abound because this is also the night of the valkyries and the banshees.

LUNAR PHASES

NEW—potentials, forward planning, new growth, conception. Attraction

FULL—magic, wishes, dreams, and desires. Manifestation

WANING/DARK—letting go, healing, psychic development, banishing, visioning. Release

LUNAR CORRESPONDENCES

DAY OF THE WEEK	*Monday*
COLORS	*white (new), silver, red (full), light blue (waning), black (banishings and dark moon)*
MINERAL	*silver*
CRYSTAL	*pearl, moonstone, clear quartz, shells, water and river stones*
DIRECTION	*West*
ELEMENT	*Water*
NUMBER	*3, 9, and 13*
TREES	*willow, aspen, eucalyptus, pear, driftwood*
FLOWERS	*jasmine, camelia, lotus, lilies, camphor, sandalwood, freshwater and ocean plants, reeds, poppy, night scented blooms, watercress, and all white flowers*
AROMA	*coconut, sandalwood, eucalyptus, camphor*
ANIMALS	*hare, hound, wolf, bat, fox, bear, cat, owl, toad, frog, lioness, serpent, snail*
MYTHICAL CREATURES	*unicorn, moonhare*
DEITIES	*Artemis, Nimue, Cybele, Diana, Isis, Arianrhod, Selene, Aradia, Hecate, Nanna, Thoth, Cerridwen*
SIGIL OF THE MOON	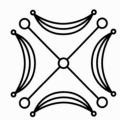
ELEMENTAL SPIRITS	*Undines, for emotional maturity and developed perceptions*

A GREATER SABBAT RITUAL: SAMHAIN

Samhain is the festival of remembering the ancestors, marking the end of the Celtic year and the dawning of the new year, and honors the last of the harvest festivals for the year just passing. The crops are in and the days become ever shorter and darker. Since this night (October 31) rests on the threshold between the old and new year, it is considered to reside between the worlds. Thus, the veils that separate spirit from matter are thinner and more easily crossed than at other times of year. This is an ideal night for divination as well as for remembrance.

❶ Set up your Wiccan altar with black and orange colors, black candles, a bell, and one white pillar candle. Add a skull or bones, pictures of departed loved ones, a jack o' lantern, and any divination tools you have (such as tarot cards, crystal ball, or runes).

❷ Light your two black candles (see opposite) and open your circle in the usual way.

❸ Go back to your altar, light your white pillar candle, ring your bell ceremoniously, and say, "*Light of Spirit, I bid you welcome. Come to the circle to bless all souls departed.*" Sit in contemplation for at least five minutes with memories of your loved ones, of the ancestors you never knew, and of your origins at the dawn of human life. Consider your lineage and what might have happened before you existed. Then give thanks back through time to all of your relations whose unions meant that you now have life. Ring the bell again when this feels completed. You can

sit, kneel, or stand before your altar during this activity. If you are performing divination, begin that now or go to Step Five.

❹ Take up your divination tool(s) and walk to all four quarters of the Circle. Stop at each one saying, "*Guardians of the North, [East, South, West], open may the doorway be to the mystic realms beyond this mortal shore. Grant this night the eyes of one that sees, 'tis time to read the signs you bring once more!*" You can perform your divination now.

❺ Give thanks for your guidance, and say, "*Light of Spirit, may souls in conflict rise in peace with you, may all those lost find their way home to you, and may your blessings be upon us all. Fare thee well.*" Extinguish your pillar candle.

You can now close your Wiccan circle as usual. Make sure you ring a bell to mark the closing, which will ensure that all spirits have departed.

A GREATER SABBAT RITUAL: IMBOLC

Imbolc, the dawn of Spring, begins on the eve of February 2. Traditionally, candle-lit processions gather at sacred wells and springs. We bless the waters that give us life and welcome in the maiden. She who gave birth to the new sun king at the winter solstice is now ready to turn the Wheel to another season. At Imbolc she is the virgin bride returning to Earth to prepare herself for her Lord's seed that will provide the harvest in the coming year. *Imbolc* (meaning "in the womb" in Gaelic) represents the stirrings of new life.

Set up your Wiccan altar with white and pastel colors, and a small bowl of almonds. The shape of the almonds symbolically represents the vagina or divine entrance to the womb of life. Spring flowers, especially snowdrops, can be included. A corn dolly or a small figurative doll dressed in white should also be put on the altar in a little cradle-shaped container filled with hay, wheat, or corn stalks. A small wand should also be crafted for the doll and left in the cradle. Sweet offerings can be placed beside the cradle in a bowl.

❶ Do not light your two altar candles yet, but open the circle as usual in every respect.

❷ Dedicate your Imbolc ritual to the virgin Goddess by saying:

*"Babe in the cradle.
Maid at the door
Gifts from the goddess
awaken once more
in the seed and the
grain and the gentle
spring rain."*

Knock on something to imitate a knock at the door. If there is more than one person present at this

ritual, a person dressed in white can actually knock at a closed door that another person can open.

"A' welcome fair maid, come in, now, come in."

Lead your spring maiden from the door to the altar or, if on your own, sweep your hands from the direction of your front door toward the babe on the altar.

❸ Light your two altar candles now and sit quietly for a few moments. Consider the light of spring returning to the Earth to warm the ground and prepare it for the planting. Each person present now takes an almond kernel and, holding it in their hand, contemplates the gifts of new life that the maiden brings. Place the almond(s) in the cradle. Add the gifts from your offering bowl that you have either made or bought especially for the spring maiden (such as violets, snowdrops, little rosewater biscuits, or seashells), sending love to the babe as you place them in the cradle.

❹ Write a wish for something you would like to manifest or birth in your own life in the central portion of the vesica symbol of fertility (shown below) you've drawn onto snippets of paper. Take up the maiden's wand and tap it three times over your wish, and then lay it gently in the cradle.

Close your circle, but leave the babe and the cradle on the altar overnight. In the morning, gather up all the grasses and offerings (including the wishes) and bury them together in some fertile soil.

By writing your wish within a vesica you are symbolically "planting" it as a seed in the womb of your life.

A GREATER SABBAT RITUAL: BELTAINE

B eltaine, a most magical festival and the third of the spring fertility celebrations on the Wiccan Wheel of the Year, begins at sunset on April 30—the day before May 1. Green and vibrant are the meadows and trees, filled with promise, life, and vitality. The nature spirits sparkle everywhere in joyful celebration of the return of their floral and leafy dwellings. Now is the time to celebrate the magic, to call for new relationships, for joy, for fertility, for the blessing of unions with a hand-fasting, and for the acknowledging of relationship endings with a hand-parting.

It is traditional for couples to jump the Beltaine Fire together, especially if they wish to conceive.

If weather permits, perform this ritual in the woods or meadows. For this ritual, you will need a stick that is painted with red and white stripes and hung with red and white ribbons and bells (topped with an optional pine cone). You also need a small bowl of sesame or sunflower seeds. Display hawthorn sprigs, violets, or pansies, and wear ivy tendrils. Burn candles in lanterns hung from the trees. Traditional folk music and drumming can be an accompaniment.

❶ Set up a natural altar with a flat-topped stone, bedecked with greenery. Place on it your decorated wand, a chalice filled with water, and oatcakes (or other unprocessed, plain, grain cracker such as water biscuits or graham crackers.) If possible, prepare wood so a small bonfire can be lit after the ritual. Open your circle.

❷ Dedicate your ritual to the Goddess and the Green Man by saying:

"*Lady of the Hills and Meadows, Lord of Nature's mantle green*
We gather on the eve of May to bless our Sacred King and Queen
Whose fertile seeds..."

Beltaine is traditionally celebrated outside in woods and meadows. Hanging lanterns from trees during evening or nighttime rituals creates a very magical atmosphere.

Cast your seeds upon and around the altar.

"*...and tender rain...*"

Take up the chalice and walk in a circle around the stone, flicking it with water.

"*...unite as lovers once again.*"

Pick up your decorated wand and turn it between your palms so that the ribbons swirl and the bells tinkle.

"*Hearken, for their sighs of love do whisper through the greening grove.*"

❸ Take up your drum, rattle, penny whistle, or musical instrument and play and dance in a spiral motion away from and toward the stone altar in the middle, giving your energy to the earth and to the union of the Lady and Lord. You can play taped music if you prefer. Once your spiral dance is completed, you can light your bonfire. Throw oatcakes into the flames, dedicating each one to appease any wrathful gods and feed the pleasure of the kindly ones. You can also throw in oatcakes for Bel (a sun god associated with Beltaine) and the Lady and Lord.

❹ Ash from the Beltaine fire can be collected once it is cooled and kept for fertility rituals and protection from harm. Traditionally the animals were also led through the ashes with invocations to protect them, as well. As soon as the fire is safe to jump, you can leap across if you wish.

A GREATER SABBAT RITUAL: LUGHNASADH

Lughnasadh, the first of three Wiccan harvest festivals, begins on the eve of August 1. Named after the warrior sun god, Lugh, it is the time for taking Oaths, signing contracts, showing feats of strength, playing games, and celebrating. Appeals to Lugh were for good weather until the harvest was safely home.

As with Beltaine, Lughnasadh is a traditional time for unions; it falls nine months before Beltaine. Since only couples with a child could "marry" in ancient days, it is likely that couples who joined together at Lughnasadh and were still childless by Beltaine would perform a hand-parting rather than a hand-fasting.

For this ritual, you will need berries from the hedgerows and trees, bread or small cakes, some corn or wheat stalks, apples, and nuts.

❶ Set up your altar with fruits, corn, nuts, apples, bread, and berries. Also include orange altar candles, approximately 18 inches (46 cm) of orange

40

Then say, "*Lord Lugh we bid you a hearty welcome at our feast.*" Raise the chalice and pour a small amount of fluid over the harvest plate. Take a sip yourself, and then pass the chalice around to any others present. All say, "*Hale and Welcome Lord.*"

❸ Light the eight votive candles and say:

"*The sun wheel turns and turns again,
Light, bright on fields of grain.
Harvest now the seeds we've sown
In colors of the Mother grown.
Now we gather what we reap.*"

Take up your ears of corn or grain and say:

"*Weep not Grain Mother, for pending sleep
shall bring you rest and comfort deep.
We shall hold you until Spring
and you return to weave and spin
new life within the seed and grain.
Weep not Grain Mother as your Sun Lord wanes
for the wheel it turns and turns again.*"

Bind the stalks with orange cord and keep this harvest bundle on an altar until the Spring. It represents a home for the Grain Mother during the winter months.

❹ Consider the passing year and be thankful for your life. Consider, too, what has not come to pass and let it go. You can make commitments to a partner, and make promises of things you will try to achieve. Close your circle.

Take your harvest offerings outside for the wildlife. Play games and be joyful.

cord, some ochre and brown colors, and a circular plate full of harvest crops. A chalice should be placed in the center (containing either mead, cider, or apple juice), with eight unlit votive candles arranged around it. Open your circle.

❷ Dedicate your ritual to the harvest and to Lord Lugh and the Grain Mother by saying:

"*Here do we gather together in joy, as we prepare to bring in the harvest of the year just lived.*" Take up the bread/cakes/berries and say, "*We give thanks to our Grain Mother for her wondrous bounty.*" Break the bread or offering over the harvest plate. All say, "*Hale and Welcome Lady.*" Share a morsel each.

LUNAR ESBATS

Esbats provide opportunities for meetings either as an individual or as a coven throughout the year for teaching, healing, and education beyond the more ceremonial and religious tones of the sabbats. An esbat is usually fixed to fall on or around a full moon or a new moon, and so can provide the opportunity for up to thirteen meetings each year (or about one a month). A focus for each meeting is planned in advance (such as understanding the runes, personal responsibility, or earth healing). Any subject that pertains to wisdom is appropriate. Attendees then contribute whatever they can to the event, or simply come to learn by absorbing the teachings.

Healing is offered to those who have asked for it. If the event is a coven esbat, questions are answered by the High Priestess or Priest. There is also a period of reflection or meditation.

The Goddess and Horned God are honored in some way, usually with cakes and ale—edible and drinkable offerings that have been blessed before ingestion.

Drawing down the moon

A few days before the full moon, consider what teachings your evening will focus upon and gather books, magazine articles, or perhaps even invite a friend who is knowledgeable in your chosen subject.

Prepare your selected area to make it magical and create a special mood with candles, lanterns, crystals, flowers, greenery, magical icons, and anything else that inspires you. Place a circular mirror (available from hardware stores) in a bowl of spring water on your altar to represent the moon. Place a clear quartz crystal on the mirror.

❶ Open your circle and then dedicate the evening to the Queen of Heaven—the moon. Light three white votive candles in your moon bowl, and say:

"Blessed Light of Night, I honor you, Mother Moon."

❷ Perform the Triple Goddess Salutation in three movements as follows:

Stand with your arms cupped upward at your shoulders in a "U" shape. Bring your arms up over your head with each hand in a "C" shape, and then cross your wrists, with your hands still making a "C" shape outward. Keeping your wrists crossed, bring them down to your heart. Then bring your arms down toward the ground and sweep each palm outward, face downward, over the Earth beneath you.

❸ Meditate for about five minutes upon the light and qualities of the moon descending into your moon bowl, focusing your love and healing thoughts into the bowl as well.

❹ Pour some of this water into your chalice. After offering some to the Goddess's libation bowl, take a sip of the moon water yourself. You can put some of this moon water in a bottle and offer it as a drink to anyone who has asked for healing.

You can now extinguish your votive candles and thank the Moon Mother. Then carry on with the evening's chosen teaching subject before closing the circle.

THE WICCAN CALENDAR

WICCA AS A PATH
TO SELF-DEVELOPMENT

*"The Veil of Isis sevenfold, to he as gauge shall be
Wherethrough clear eyed he shall behold the ancient Mystery."*

VOICES OF THE SOUL, V. J. DALEY

A*ll witches take an Oath at their first degree that marks their initiation into the Craft. They thereby swear to harm none, to live in perfect love and perfect trust, to work on developing themselves to a greater understanding of their true nature, and to act unselfishly for the benefit of all. With these promises in place, the witch begins the journey of a lifetime. It is the most wondrous journey of all because they are working to uncover their own true nature. Solitary witches can still approach some covens to ask for initiation as a witch without obligation to join a coven (see front of book for Wiccan services).*

In Wicca, self-development does not happen through grabbing power and prestige, nor is it gained by simply "looking the part." It is achieved through dedication and devotion to the seeking of wisdom, love, and awareness. The magic is only revealed to those who are willing to grow. The Wiccan way opens you to the most profound understandings that can only ever be experienced personally. Wicca is an oral tradition for this reason. It cannot ever be an intellectual exercise. Unless you have prepared yourself and advanced in your spiritual integrity, you will not have the experiences. Magic is everywhere—in the stones, the stars, the streams, and the seasons. Just for a moment, contemplate the fact that you are on a small rock that is hurtling through space en route to the edges of eternity. Is Creation to you not the most incredible mystery? Learning to resonate with these universal truths within our own spirit is part of the magic. This chapter will help you to begin to raise your awareness toward those magical realms that you hold within your soul.

THE THREE DEGREES OF ADVANCEMENT

Within Wicca there are Three Degrees of advancement. The First Degree is bestowed on an individual at the point of initiation as a witch to mark them joining the Craft. At this stage the initiate is called a Priest or Priestess. Advancement in personal and spiritual understanding prepares the initiate for the Second Degree. When they feel ready they ask for this initiation. Second Degree witches are called High Priests and High Priestesses, and at this stage a female can start her own coven. The Third Degree is the most difficult to attain and is considered the degree of perfection as a Wiccan. Third Degree witches will not reveal their grade publicly. All three degrees require personal effort, dedication, and spiritual attainment.

Only those with true courage can succeed in progressing successfully through the Three Degrees. It is only by working on ourselves and by striving for wisdom, love, and truth that our souls can develop. A vital part of Wiccan teaching, therefore, is self-development. The exercise that follows will help you to open to your greater self and free your Spirit from the limitations of the mundane world.

A self-development meditation

Always have a lighted candle during this exercise, which represents the illumined Spirit. It invites the presence of the powers of transformation that are held within the Fire element. This exercise is best performed in the morning because of its energizing qualities. It is a powerful meditation, so you should allow at least ten minutes after you finish to readjust back to everyday consciousness.

❶ Light frankincense incense and let the smoke waft around you and your space. If you like, gently breathe in the incense. Perform the Fourfold Breath (see page 49) for a few minutes. Remain standing.

❷ Visualize a star of purest light high above your head. From this star is a beam of whitest light. It descends in a column of brightness, sparkling with flecks of tiny silver and gold particles, going through the top of your head and down toward the Earth and around your body. Feel the column of light passing down through you and all around you (see opposite).

❸ Feel the light touching any shadows, blocks, and tensions within your body, allowing them to be replaced by the sparkling light as it descends slowly through you. Imagine that the shadows are being gently pushed out through openings in the soles of your feet and down into the Earth.

❹ When your body and spirit feel cleansed, rejuvenated, and filled with light, close the openings in your feet. Let your whole body be filled and encircled with light for a few minutes. Let the column of light return back up to the star and on an out breath slowly open your eyes.

BREATHING TECHNIQUES

For thousands of years, many traditions have considered the breath to be a doorway to the mysteries. Wicca also respects the breath as a magical tool. By understanding and working consciously with the breath, we can raise our awareness, release stress, balance our energy, and connect to our spirit. Some Wiccans have the ability to raise the wind or heal through chanting into wounds. Both are Air Element gifts, and our breathing is the physical connection to it. We can only survive without air for a few moments. It is our most vital connection to the forces that give us life.

You can use these breathing techniques to calm yourself, release fears and anxieties, prepare yourself for magical work, and connect to your spirit.

Peace breathing

Peace breathing can be used when you wish to calm stresses and emotions, and when you wish to release something.

❶ Find a warm and comfortable spot. Either lie down with a pillow beneath your head, or choose a suitable straight-backed chair where your feet can easily touch the floor. Turn off telephones and ensure that you will not be disturbed for at least fifteen minutes.

❷ Set a timer for fifteen minutes. Place it beneath a cushion so it will not startle you when it rings. Lie down or arrange yourself in your chosen chair.

❸ Place your hands on your stomach. As you breathe in, attempt to push your hands out as if you were blowing up a balloon in your stomach and pushing your belly out. This ensures that you are breathing deeply. Breathe in as far as you can, but do not hold your breath. Imagine that you are inhaling peace throughout your body (see opposite).

❹ Keeping your hands on your stomach, heave a big sigh. Let the out breath go as completely as you can until you cannot breathe out any more air. On this out breath, visualize that you are releasing all tension, stress, emotion, or anxiety. Relax your muscles with each out breath and simply let the in breath come when it does. Continue until the alarm rings.

❺ Upon completion, stretch your limbs. Then open your eyes on an out breath. Turn on one side and get up very slowly from the floor, or rise from the chair carefully.

CHAPTER FOUR

48

The fourfold breath

You can use this breath to raise your awareness and to prepare for all magical work. Called the Fourfold Breath as mentioned on page 14, it is a magical breathing technique.

❶ Find a comfortable spot (sitting or lying down) and ensure you will not be disturbed for about five minutes.

❷ Breathe in to the count of four, hold your breath for the count of four, breathe out to the count of four, and then hold your breath for the count of four. Find a way to balance the timing of your breathing by repeating something (such as "one manitou,"* "two manitou," and so on).

* ***manitou*** = *a supernatural force that according to an Algonquian conception pervades the natural world*

UNDERSTANDING MAGICAL CORRESPONDENCES

Correspondences provide a means to focus the ingredients for your magic in a particular direction. By the way you put them together, you can achieve a desired result. The easiest way to start is to decide which day of the week best suits your magical work. Then refer to the chart to see what else you could include to complement and support your intent. Correspondences strengthen the intent, thus making it clearer for the magical realms to receive and interpret. Grasping correspondences takes time and effort, but is a necessary and vital part of ritual and magical work.

This chart gives you a sample of correspondences that will allow you to perform effective magic. Plan to perform your magic on the day of the week that best fits the magic you are going to undertake (such as Friday for love, Monday for healing, or Sunday for success). Then look along the table to see which fragrances, herbs, crystals, and deities you could work with to support your magical request. You will also notice that colors are part of the table. For example, you could use a purple cloth and purple candles when working with Jupiter on a Thursday. This table has just a handful of correspondences to get you started. It is important not to manipulate reality simply for purely indulgent reasons. Always precede your magical work with the saying, *"An it be for highest good and by Divine will . . . "*(this is an archaic way of saying "If it be for the greater good . . . ") This will indicate that you are content to accept whatever outcome is best, or the one that is part of your true destiny.

Appealing to a deity

❶ Set up your altar with the appropriate correspondences chosen in accordance with the chart opposite. Open your circle in the usual way.

❷ Drum, rattle, or dance around your circle to raise your energy. Then perform the fourfold breath for a few minutes.

❸ Repeat the following request three times while facing your altar:

"Lady/Lord . . . [state your name here], *this night/day I beseech thee, come to this Circle and hear my plea for . . .* [state the full reason for your magic, such as healing or love]. *This I pledge for highest good—hear me Lady/Lord—so mote it be!"* Ring a bell and close your circle.

CHART OF MAGICAL CORRESPONDENCES

DAY OF WEEK	MON.	TUES.	WED.	THURS.	FRI.	SAT.	SUN.
PLANET	Moon	Mars	Mercury	Jupiter	Venus	Saturn	Sun
GOVERNS	fertility, dreams, psychism, revelations, healing, emotion	conflict, power, protection	travel, study, communication	luck, fortune, law	love, friendship, relationships	obstacles, timing, land, inheritance, karma	prosperity, success, maintaining health
COLOR	white (new moon), silver/red (full moon), pale blue (waning moon), black (dark moon)	red	yellow	purple, turquoise	green, pink	black, indigo	orange, gold
GEM/CRYSTAL	clear quartz, pearl, moonstone	ruby, hematite	agate, carnelian	turquoise, amethyst	rose quartz, emerald, jade	jet, obsidian	amber, sunstone
SYMBOL/SIGIL							
HERBS	camphor, sandalwood	coriander, tobacco, garlic	caraway, marjoram	nutmeg, cinquefoil	myrtle, violet	evergreens, asafoetida	bay leaves, mistletoe, marigold
FRAGRANCE	jasmine	pine	lavender	honeysuckle, cloves	rose	cypress	frankincense
DEITIES	Diana, Isis, Selene, Hecate, Cerridwen	Woden, Ares, Thor	Thoth, Mercury, Athena	Juno, Hera, Zeus	Branwen, Aphrodite, Venus	Herne, Cronos	Lugh, Sekhmet

CHARMS

O riginating from a Latin word (*carmen*) meaning "song," charms are magically charged occult articles made by or for the wearer to avert negativity or to invite good luck. Our modern-day charm bracelet originated from this practice. Charms can be made with any ingredients as long as the magical correspondences and items we use are associated with the charm's intended purpose. A love-attracting charm would need to include ingredients associated with love (such as the colors green and pink), the goddess Aphrodite, and herbs and spices associated with love (such as myrtle, rose, or basil). Refer to the magical correspondences chart on page 51 for more details.

Making a love charm

In order to understand fully how to make effective magical charms (and in fact for any Wiccan magical practices), you will need to explore and understand correspondences. Investigate reference books on correspondences and build up the confidence to put things together that are associated with your focus. All herbs with links to love can be included in a love charm. This can be done by weaving them in, anointing the object with its fragrance or oil, or burning an herbal incense associated with love as you weave your love web. Appropriate love crystals, tree berries, spices, associated love icons, symbols, and signs can all be included. Imagination and creativity are all part of magic. There is no set way to create magical charms. Each is unique to the maker and to the needs of the wearer. Once you have your ingredients, plan your making to coincide with the next full moon.

❶ Find a willow tree in your vicinity. When the moon is full, carefully and respectfully remove an 18-inch (46-cm) young tree branch. Don't neglect to give your thanks. Soak the branch in warm water to make it flexible, if necessary.

❷ Bend the branch into a hoop and fasten the ends firmly together. Weave thin green cord or thread around and through your hoop to create a web effect. It does not have to look like a work of art.

❸ Quietly keep repeating the following love chant under your breath:

"Here I weave a web this night, filled with love and warmth and light,
Come to me my lover true, let me share love's joy with you."

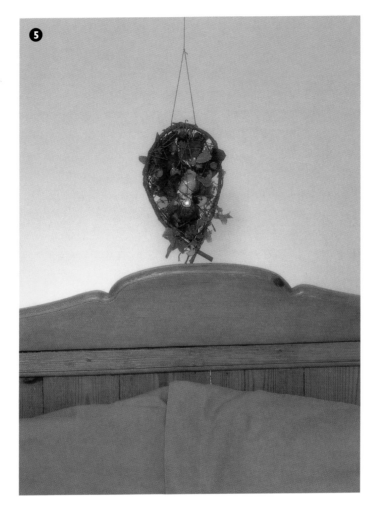

❹ Continue to weave and bind the ingredients that you have gathered into your threads, to complement and strengthen your charm's powers (such as three, seven, or nine basil leaves, paper roses, heart shapes, crescent moons, and ivy tendrils) until your charm feels suitably completed. You can also hang swan, dove, or duck feathers from your charm if you like because they are birds traditionally associated with love.

❺ Hang your charm above your bed, and every night repeat your wish for true love to find you. When fulfilled, go to the willow tree from which you had cut the branch. Bury your charm beneath it and give Mother Willow your thanks.

WICCAN SERVICE TO OTHERS

Wiccans see all human beings as potential brothers or sisters. We are all children of the Goddess and Horned God and therefore equals in their eyes. Anyone wishing to follow Wiccan ideals will therefore practice kindness, compassion, tolerance, and respect for everyone, regardless of any incompatibility or differences. Authentic Wiccans live by the ethics of integrity, honor, truth, and love as much as they are able.

Wiccan service to others can be shared on many levels, the main criteria being to care. If there is a need and we are able to help in any way, then a Wiccan would offer their services appropriately. At no time would a Wiccan interfere or take over a situation. They would simply offer support and help where asked.

Protection within a sacred circle

This magical act can be performed for others who ask for your help, or for yourself should you find you need extra protection or strength. As with all magic, the first thing you must do is to decide which is the best day of the week to weave it. For protection, the best planet to work with is Mars. Your altar, tools, and accessories should all reflect Martian powers. This would mean red candles, as well as offerings of dynamic fiery spices and herbs (such as garlic cloves, black peppercorns, tobacco, and chiles) laid out in an offering bowl.

❶ Set up your altar to your chosen planet on a Tuesday (day of Mars). Cast your circle in the usual way.

❷ Go back to your altar and take up your wand and walk around the circle. If you don't have a wand, walk around the circle with an altar candle. As you do so, say:

"By the powers of Fire, a ring of fire I make, to guard from harm, the good they do forsake. Ring of Fire keeps me [or state the name of the person requiring protection here] *safe, Ring of Fire keeps me safe, Ring of Fire keeps me safe. So mote it be!"*

❶

❸ Put your wand back on the altar. Sit, kneel, or stand before your altar, and visualize a circle of red, orange, and gold flames all around you until you feel and genuinely believe that they are strong and vibrant all around you.

❹ Pick up your spice offering bowl and visualize the ring of fire around you being drawn into your spices, activating their magical properties and filling them with protection and power. Once you feel that the flames have all moved into your spices, pack them into a little pouch or bag and give them to the person in need or carry them with you as and when you need them. Keep them close by for as long as needs be. When no longer needed, bury the pouch beneath a holly or pine tree with your thanks.

Close your circle in the usual way.

THE NATURAL WORLD

*"Earth my body, water my blood
Air my breath and fire my spirit."*

TRADITIONAL WICCAN CHANT

H ow extraordinary it is that all our needs are met by the
natural world. We have been given our food, water, shelter,
warmth, building and craft materials, clothing, and leisure
possibilities. It is even more awesome when we take into account our
human gifts of music, dance, and creativity. We really are truly blessed
to have this Earth as our home.

So many of us have lost that vital connection to the Earth, to the
simpler pleasures such as a sunset, a moonrise, or a shooting star. So
few of us consider how lucky we are to have food and water. We often
fail to appreciate our life until it changes in some way to our detriment.

This chapter explains the deep connection that Wicca has with the
natural world and describes ways to begin working more creatively
with it. We explore the four Spiritual Elements, the nature spirits, the
changing seasons, and frameworks for the seasonal festivals in the
four Greater Sabbats. The Spiritual Elements are distinct from the
chemical elements in that they are the spiritual quality of each element.
With Spiritual Water, for example, we are relating to Water's emotive,
feeling nature and not to the physicalities of flowing water or
weathered rain. The nature spirits are elemental essences from the
natural world and exist as nature's unseen or energetic presences that
we can honor and work with cooperatively in order to be shown the
magic of nature. Wicca is natural. It is nature, fertility, and the harvest.
Explore the festivals in this chapter and find the qualities of your true
nature emerging as a result.

SACRED ECOLOGY

S acred Ecology means caring for the Earth and all of her creations in a wider context than solely conservation or sustainability alone. Wiccans also recognize the spiritual beauty of life on Earth and work consciously to honor and respect all life forms, whether they be tree, animal, flower, or insect. Wiccans can be termed sacred ecologists because they strive to be guardians of the planet and see all of its kingdoms as a sacred human responsibility. The human race is destroying the ecology of the Earth rapidly and thoughtlessly. Wiccans, however, work to love and preserve the Earth not to destroy her, because she is our spiritual Mother.

If you wish to emulate these Wiccan ideals, strive to conserve the resources where you live. Care for the Earth and keep it well loved. Join local conservation projects, recycle your trash, compost as much as you can, and educate yourself about global conservation and wildlife preservation projects where you could make a contribution. Get active! Taking personal responsibility is vital. Many people ignore problems until they are right at their front door. Unfortunately, with regard to preserving this endangered planet that will simply be too late. We must act now and act swiftly. Here is what you can do to help.

Option one
Look at each room in your home and minimize trash, clutter, and any unnecessary items. Make the minimum of purchases that you actually need for your household. Decorate your home with "green" paints, environmentally friendly furniture, and "fair trade" products (products that have been bought fairly from developing countries, without exploitation). Cut down your consumerism wherever you can. Repair and reuse wherever possible.

Option two
Build a compost bin and recycle all compostable waste for reuse on your garden. Grow your own vegetables and herbs without chemicals where you can.

Option three
Buy organic products and eco-friendly cosmetics available from all good natural/organic product outlets. Join a local organic produce scheme, where you have organic vegetables delivered to your door once a week. Buy healthy items from local farmer's markets. Support local initiatives that conserve the planet's resources. Eat wisely.

Option four
Join conservation organizations, educate yourself about global issues, and refuse to support companies that damage the environment. Support environmentally friendly projects and don't use products that pollute or damage our world. Lobby local parliament or government representatives to support environmentally friendly initiatives. Let your voice be heard.

Option five

The power of prayer can be used in areas where there is a need for love and caring, but you are unable to make a physical contribution (such as a war torn country and places around the world suffering famine or drought).

Light an emerald green candle and quietly sit in daily five-minute contemplations, focusing on your chosen area. Send peace, love, and your caring thoughts into the candle flame and imagine that all darkness and suffering is being lifted and loved away. Stay calm and repeat regularly throughout your contemplations: *"An it be for highest good, may the gift of* [state the requirement here, like "water," "food," "peace"] *find those who suffer this day. Mother, Father, please aid your children as I shall aid them however I am able. Hear this plea, I beseech thee."*

EXPLORING THE FOUR SPIRITUAL ELEMENTS

The four Elements of Earth, Air, Fire, and Water are manifested in physical reality by solidity, fresh air, winds, warmth and light, rain, oceans, rivers, and lakes. These are the physical aspects of each Element. The four Elements also have qualities in the spiritual dimensions that can be used to develop a deeper spiritual and personal understanding of our true nature because we embody the spiritual qualities of each Element as well as their physical aspects.

AIR

The physical Air Element is closest to Spirit (or ether) that is the space that contains all of the spiritual and physical Elements. When Spirit descends into the physical Elements it travels from Spirit into Air, Air into Fire, Fire into Water, and Water into Earth, traveling from the most refined down to the densest. Thus to bring Spirit down to Earth, we begin with the Air Element and the qualities of Spiritual Air.

Within the air we breathe we can also find the qualities of Spiritual Air, those finer virtues so lacking in the human spirit these days—honesty, integrity, and honor.

Negative Spiritual Air

The unrefined manifestations of Spiritual Air would include negative thinking, poor communication skills, gossip, inability to learn and grow, tyranny, fear and anxiety, dishonesty, mental chaos, and psychic confusion.

Positive Spiritual Air

The pure qualities of Spiritual Air are honesty, the ability to learn and understand, integrity, clear communication, constructive thinking, honor, mental harmony, clairaudience (hearing spirit), and intellectual brightness.

The Western alchemical symbol for the Air Element.

Exploring the Spiritual Air Element

❶ Set up your altar in the East of your circle, the direction for the Air Element. Lay it out in yellow and lilac colors, with yellow candles, your athame, agates, amethysts, and/or turquoise crystals, hazel fronds, violets and lavender flowers, a Thoth statue or picture, and burn lavender incense. Lay your athame on the altar between the candles.

❷ Light your altar candles and then cast your circle. Kneel or sit before your altar, holding your athame toward it and invoke Mighty Thoth (te-ho-teh), an ancient Egyptian deity associated with Air's teachings *"Mighty Thoth—with you I breathe the Spirit of Air into my being. Teach me, Lord, the ways of truth, honor, and understanding. Breathe your wisdom into me and help me embody my greater self."*

❸ Draw a large upward facing "A"-shaped triangle with your athame in the air before you with a line across its center and visualize Thoth

(the ibis-headed deity) standing the other side of the triangle as if it were a doorway. Breathe in through the triangle imagining the purest qualities of Spiritual Air filling your lungs and body. Breathe out any impurities or lower Spiritual Air Element attributes you feel you have back through the triangle toward Thoth. Honesty with self is vital at this point. Continue for at least five minutes.

❹ Give thanks to Thoth for his presence, and pledge that you will strive to be honorable from that point on. Close your circle.

FIRE

The physical aspects of the Fire Element are warmth and light. The fire of the sun is central to Creation for without it there would be no life. The spiritual essence of the Fire Element does not consist of the physical flames that we see with the naked eye. It is a vital energetic and vibrant force that brings courage, strength, and valor. Spiritual Fire is transformative—moving the seeker to greater consciousness by "burning away" those things that no longer serve us well. In terms of masculine and feminine, the Fire Element represents the male and in magic is considered an active rather than a passive force.

Spiritual Fire, like when making a real fire, requires a sacrifice of some kind. The tree; its branches, the candle flame; its waxen body. With humans, for example, cowardice must be sacrificed for bravery to emerge.

Negative Spiritual Fire

When being met by lower frequencies in the soul, Spiritual Fire can produce aggression, domination, cowardice, temper, erratic behavior, unpredictability, and egotism.

Positive Spiritual Fire

The purest qualities of Spiritual Fire are courage, valor, inner conviction, joy, strength, humility, compassion, passion, and transformation.

Exploring the Spiritual Fire Element

❶ Set up your altar in the south of your Circle and lay out your altar to the Fire Element by including reds, oranges and/or golds in your color scheme, with two orange altar candles, one pillar candle in gold, marigolds, your wand, oak leaves, cloves, orange crystals like carnelians, and amber, and burn cedar incense or frankincense. Also have nearby a fireproof container, matches, and small pieces of paper and a pen. Lions, phoenixes, and salamanders can be displayed as well.

The Western alchemical symbol for the Fire Element.

❷ Light your altar candles and cast your circle. Light your gold pillar candle and take it and stand in the South of your circle facing outward. Hold out your candle and say:

"Here do I call for the Spirit of Fire to illuminate my being. Lords of the spiritual Sun, come hither to lighten my shadows and brighten my soul. In you I entrust my Spirit."

❸ Take your pillar candle back to your altar and place it in the center. Sit before your altar and consider carefully and deeply what you need to

sacrifice in order to transform yourself to a greater self. Write down on a piece of paper a single Fire-based word that sums up what you will give to the Spiritual essence of Fire via the candle flame, such as anger, or egotism perhaps.

❹ Before casting your pieces of paper into the gold candle flame, gather up as much of the particular limitation from inside yourself as you can before giving it to the Fire. Once lit, drop it into your heatproof container and leave to burn to ashes completely. Give thanks to the Sun Lords, and close your circle in the usual way.

❸

WATER

CHAPTER FIVE

The physical Water Element flows across most of the Earth and our bodies contain over 75 percent of it. We birth in physical form from the waters of a womb. The Spiritual Water Element presides over the emotions, the feelings, and perceptions. It is flowing by nature and teaches us how to be flexible and adaptable. Just as physical water cleanses, quenches, and cultivates the land, so Spiritual Water brings us opportunities to cleanse emotions, quench our spiritual thirst, and cultivate our inner being with love. The Water Element represents the female and in magical work is considered a passive rather than an active force.

The Water Element also governs sleep, dreams, psychism, and relationships of all kinds.

Negative Spiritual Water

Spiritual Water when hindered by blocks in the soul will induce over-emotionalism, reactionary behavior, stagnation, insecurity, doubt, inflexibility, depression, and mood swings.

Positive Spiritual Water

The purest expression of Spiritual Water is love, flexibility, adaptability, cooperation, clarity, developed intuition, serenity, and grace.

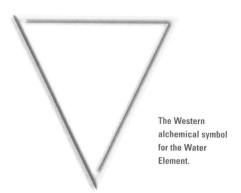

The Western alchemical symbol for the Water Element.

Exploring the Spiritual Water Element

The Spiritual Water Element helps us to develop clear boundaries, clarity of purpose and direction, and understanding of our inner feelings.

❶ Lay out your altar in the West of your circle to the Water Element with blue, silver, and white colors and two blue candles. Add a bowl of water in the center containing water habitat flowers such as a lily or iris; your chalice; jasmine flowers; icons of water creatures like dolphins, otters, whales, or seahorses; clear quartz crystals; moonstones; or shells. Moon icons are also appropriate, plus an indoor fountain and an Isis statue if you wish. Calming, rhythmical music can also be played.

❷ Cast your circle and light your altar candles. Standing facing your altar, pick up your chalice (that is, ideally, filled with spring water from a sacred well), and invoke the Lady Isis to come and join you by saying, *"Blessed Lady of Grace, I stand before you as your child. Help me to understand the Sacred ways that flow from you unto my heart. Cleanse my Spirit Lady, let love touch my soul and heal its sorrows. So mote it be!"*

❸ Put your chalice back on your altar, place your hands across your chest over your heart, and close your eyes. Meditate in this position upon your inner feelings, fears, doubts, insecurities. Let tears flow if they come for tears are the language of the heart. Contemplate whatever troubles you. Continue for at least five minutes this way. Uncross your arms and cup them upward at shoulder height and ask Lady Isis to lift them from you into the chalice. Open your eyes and gaze upon the water flower and consider its beauty, for you too carry that beauty in your soul.

❹ Give your thanks to Lady Isis for her presence, close your circle in the usual way, and take your chalice water to tip into a lake or river.

EARTH

The Earth Element in its physical manifestation provides us with the material world, with all matter, food, vegetation, and species. These are the physical aspects of the Earth Element. Spiritual Earth invites us to wisdom and understanding, to making connections and realizing our place in Creation, and to honoring and respecting the Earth, to being reliable, to embodying all the best attributes of a Mother Goddess full of unconditional love. The Earth Element is defined as feminine and in magical terms is considered passive.

As with all things we have the choice whether we move in negative or positive ways with Earth's spiritual potential.

Negative Spiritual Earth

The baser, more negative translation of Spiritual Earth energy within our characters would include obstinacy, stubbornness, sexual dysfunction, insecurity, inflexibility, belligerence, unreliability, meanness, laziness, and sloth.

Positive Spiritual Earth

The highest qualities of Spiritual Earth would include wisdom, stability, reliability, protection and strength in adversity, self-defense, endurance, clairsentience (sensing/feeling spirit), nourishment and abundance. Wiccans work with the Earth Element when needing to protect someone psychically, because of its abilities to earth and stabilize unwanted or overcharged energy.

The Western alchemical symbol for the Earth Element.

Exploring the Spiritual Earth Element

❶ Set up your altar in the North, with Earth Element correspondences of green or black candles, a bowl of clean earth or natural sea salt, fossils, ferns, root vegetables, and any black or green stones or crystals you may have. Burn cypress oil in an aromatherapy burner on your altar as well.

❷ Light your candles and then cast your circle. Take a pinch of earth/salt into the palm of each hand. Holding the essence Earth make the following invocation to Gaia (the Earth Mother):

"Mother, I come to remember the spirit of Earth within my being. I ask that you guide me to its wisdom, to the spiritual teachings held within your Sacred Earth. So mote it be!"

❸ Consider your character carefully and be totally honest with yourself about who you feel you really are and how you behave in life.

Allow the essence of the Earth that you hold in the palms of your hands to enter your being and guide you to places within yourself that hold negative Spiritual Earth, such as perhaps you know you are a little unreliable. Allow the spirit of Earth's higher qualities to energetically move any negative Earth you have into the physical Earth that you hold in your hands. Feel that space being replaced by the dignity of Spiritual Earth. When you are finished, place the earth/salt back into the bowl.

❹ Pledge that you will strive to raise yourself to a greater good within your spiritual being, give thanks to Gaia for her presence, and close your circle. Take your bowl of earth/salt outside and respectfully sprinkle it over the ground (avoiding greenery if using salt) visualizing whatever negative Earth you placed in the physical earth/salt being transmuted into food for new life.

NATURE AND THE ELEMENTALS

Elemental Spirits

Wiccans believe that all physical Elements have spiritual counterparts that are presided over by their Elemental Spirits. For Air it is the Sylphs, for Fire it is the Salamanders, for Water it is the Undines and for Earth it is the Gnomes. These are the spirits of the four elements.

Creating an Elementals nature garden

If you have a garden, you can honor the Elemental spirits there. For the Sylphs include bells, chimes, and things that move in the breeze in the East of your garden. For the Salamanders include lanterns, votive candles, fairy lights, and things that reflect rays of sunlight (such as metal disks) in the South of your garden. For the Undines include water fountains, ponds, decorative shells, clear crystals, and water plants in the West of your garden. For the Gnomes include mosses and lichens, wild plants and flowers, herbs, fallen tree bark, rocks, stones, and fossils in the North of your garden. If you do not have a garden, create a magical area in your home by miniaturizing these suggestions and arranging them on a tray or large shallow bowl. Regularly tend it and love it to show the Elementals you care.

Invoking the Elemental Spirits

Stand facing the Elemental direction you wish to invoke and adapt the following in each case: *"[Eastward] I stand to honor you [Sylphs] Spirits of [Air]. Bless the breath of life [Air], light [Fire], love [Water], wisdom [Earth]) that you bring. May our spirits fly [Air], shine [Fire], flow [Water], walk [Earth] together always. So mote it be!"*

Nature Spirits

Nature Spirits are slightly different from Elemental Spirits in that they are specific to trees, plants, herbs, and flowers rather than the four Elements of Air, Fire, Water, and Earth. The Dryads are tree spirits, and the Devas are flower spirits, all held within the embrace of our Mother and Father, the Goddess and Horned God.

Meeting Nature Spirits

Many human beings in the west today have lost their vital connection to nature and the natural world, to the point where they no longer feel part of it or in any way reliant upon it. This is not the case. Without nature we cease to exist. Learn to honor what supports and nourishes you and take time to respect, preserve, and enhance all life on Earth. Meeting with nature spirits enables human beings to become more attuned to nature and to the planet that sustains us.

❶ Choose to meet with either a Dryad or a Deva by selecting your tree or flower first. This can be absolutely any one to which you feel drawn.

❷ Settle yourself and your energy before approaching your chosen flora and announcing your presence and intention. Place a little gift or offering of a piece of your hair, a small crystal, or perhaps dried fruit, by your flora and then say:

"Dryad of this Sacred tree, I ask you now reveal to me, the hallowed place in which you dwell, how may I learn to know you well?"

OR

"Deva of this blessed flower, gentle spirit come to me now to teach my heart the Sacred way, and live in beauty every day."

❷

Touch the tree trunk carefully, or cup your hands gently around your flower and close your eyes. Breathe peacefully and without expectation for a while.

❸ A Nature Spirit should appear in your thoughts if you are quiet and peaceful enough. They will talk with you mentally, guide you and answer any questions you may have. If your heart is in the right place, the spirits will always honor you by their presence.

THE NATURAL WORLD

Respecting the natural world

If we wish the secrets of nature to be revealed
to us, we must be prepared to give something of
ourselves, such as our time and energy. Too often
we take without giving and gratitude, and this
includes our attitudes to Nature. Mother Nature
is finite. Without our sincerity, care, and respect,
she will never reveal her magic, nor touch us with
her grace.

Communing with spirits of place

Every environment and habitat has its Spirit of
Place or Guardian, whether indoors or out. Here is
how you can begin to be respectful of habitats and
seek connection with them.

❶ Take yourself to a place of your choice and
breathe in the air, feel the earth beneath your feet,
and speak your intent to the local spirit:

"Spirit of Place, Guardian Spirit, I come in peace."

Knock your staff on the ground three times and
then say,

"Grant me entrance to your domain."

Wait a while for your answer, leaves rustling,
a robin or bird flying by, sun breaking out from
clouds, or perhaps even a shadow passing.

❷ Move with dignity and deference in that
habitat, open your mind to the mysteries hidden

there, and let yourself be led and guided by the
Guardian Spirit through its domain. There may well
be a gift of a feather, seedpod, or rare plant
waiting for you to commune with. (Please don't
pick endangered species.) Be open and trusting
of the Guardian Spirit.

❸ When you are leaving the chosen place, turn to
face where you have been, bow your head and say,

*"Guardian Spirit, your honor is mine honor. Thank
you for guiding me through. Now I must leave you.
Farewell."*

Seeking answers from nature

All creatures, birds, and insects live in the domain of Nature as well as trees, crops, and vegetation. We can learn so much by simply being with her, for we too are part of the natural world. When we are coming from the right place within ourselves, Mother Nature will send messengers to answer questions and ease a troubled mind.

❶ Formulate your question clearly and concisely in your mind and feelings. Take yourself and your staff outside to somewhere you feel safe and secure. Hilltops and sacred circles or sites are the most ideal.

❷ Draw a clockwise circle above your head with your staff and invoke the Mother Goddess and Father Horned God thus:

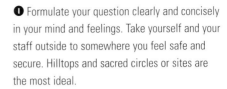

*"In the names of the
Goddess and Great
Horned God,
I cast this sphere
upon the Winds.
Come heed my call
I beseech thee, help me,
guide me, teach me."*

❸ Wait and watch, for somewhere something will come to you. Perhaps a bird, an insect, or your eyes will be drawn to a small flower in the grass, maybe a passing creature rustling nearby, or cloud formations. Let its message be received by your spirit and trust that your intuition will understand the answer if you are patient and open to it. There are many reference books that give meanings to the messages of birds, creatures, and plants if you need to refer to words.

THE SEASONS

Each season has its place on the Wiccan wheel of the year. Spring is in the east, Summer is in the south, Fall is in the west, and Winter is in the north. This is a symbolic depiction of the seasons that helps us to describe or define the seasonal variations within a circle.

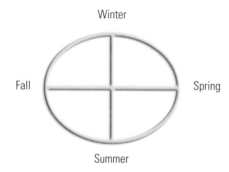

Winter

Fall · Spring

Summer

As each season rises and falls, so the rhythms of nature also rise and fall within us. Our lives are similar to the four seasons. The baby, the child, the adult, and the elder are like the spring, summer, fall, and winter of our own existence. Nature ebbs and flows throughout each year bringing new life, nurturing it, providing the fruits, and finally releasing everything back into the Earth. Then the whole cycle begins again.

The table below provides a seasonal example of correspondences. We need to understand the maps we make with our magic so that our intentions and focus are clear. In spring, the most potent time for magical work is the dawn of the day with the athame. Therefore if you specifically wish to honor the spring season, you would include dawn and the athame as well as perhaps violet and yellow flowers and candles. The fall season would involve sunset and the chalice, and so on.

Each season can provide us with opportunities to explore our humanity. In spring, for example, when the eggs are fertilized and new life stirs in the seeds, we can consider what new ideas we might like to bring into being in our coming year. It is the time to plant our life seeds and ideas, utilizing the spring correspondences below.

SEASONAL CORRESPONDENCES

SEASON	DIRECTION	TIME OF DAY	COLORS	ELEMENT	TOOL	FLOWER
SPRING	East	dawn	yellow/violet	Air	athame	lavender
SUMMER	South	midday	red/green	Fire	wand	marigold
FALL	West	dusk	blue/orange	Water	chalice	cornflower
WINTER	North	midnight	black/white	Earth	pentagram	pine

In summer, when nature is rampant and growing fast, it is the time for the manifestation of those ideas that we planted in the spring. The seeds of our labors should be starting to show in some way in our lives at some practical or visible level.

Fall is the time of the harvest. We should be able to "harvest" the fruits of our labors from the seeds we planted in the spring or, in other words, gain some kind of results. It is also the time to prune back and/or release those seeds (ideas or plans) that did not or could not manifest for us in that year. We should either leave them alone or plan to replant them as new ideas in the following spring.

Spring/Air—flying creatures
Summer/Fire—busy, active creatures
Fall/Water—creatures of hunt and harvest
Winter/Earth—earth and night dwelling creatures like moles and bats

In the winter, we can envision what it is that we would like to achieve in the year that is to come. Rest is necessary. It provides a break between cycles, giving us the time to contemplate and consider potential courses of action. The more we can learn to follow these patterns that are revealed in nature, the more in tune with nature we will become.

SPRING

All of the Celtic festivals begin at sunset on the day before the actual date and run until sunset on the actual date. At the dawn of Spring—on the eve of February 2—the first of three Wiccan fertility festivals heralds the return of the virgin goddess to the Earth. Now we bless the wells and springs, cleanse and clear our environments, and welcome the beginning of the new season. Keywords are *purity, innocence, cleansing, new beginnings,* and *growth.*

Making sacred incense

It is advisable to make specific magical blends during the actual season when you can gather ingredients as they ripen. This ensures that the flavors and fragrances of that time of year are at their most potent.

Spring correspondences

White, pastel colors, the veil, snowdrops, lilies, rowan trees, seashells, primroses, violets, white candles.

Direction—East
Magical Tool—Athame
Time of Day—Dawn

When you make up your own blends of incense, you concentrate more of your energy and intent into the ritual or magical event when you burn them. Because incense is one of the Air Element's representations, making mixtures is an ideal activity to undertake during the spring season. Spring is the time on the Wiccan wheel of the year that is associated with the Air Element. However, seasonal incenses can be made throughout the whole year.

❶ Gather the ingredients you need either at dawn on February 2 or in the early evening of February 1. Decorate your altar with a bowl of spring water, irises, snowdrops, rowan sprigs, seashells, violets, primroses, and white candles. If you like, choose a swathe of white or pastel veil material that you can wear over your head.

❷ Set your altar in the Eastern quarter of your circle with your incense ingredients and a pestle and mortar. Open your circle in the usual way. Place your veil over your head and close your eyes for a moment. Hold your palms out to your herbs on the altar and call for the virgin goddess to bless your ingredients by saying:

"Upon this night,
bless Lady Bright
these herbs of spring,
to welcome in
the Bride."

❸ In accordance with the recipe that follows, put your myrrh grains into a mortar, and use a pestle to grind them into smaller grains. Add the angelica, lavender flowers, and finely chopped bay leaves and continue to grind them together. Add nine drops of lemon verbena oil. Finally, add your snowdrop flower heads and mix gently.

- 1 tsp angelica herb
- 1 tsp dried lavender flowers
- 3 bay leaves, finely chopped
- 9 drops lemon verbena oil
- 2 tsp myrrh grains
- snowdrop flowers (optional)

❹ Pour your mix into an airtight jar and then place it back on your altar. Lift your veil, take up your athame, place the blade over the jar, and say:

"'Tis made for the maiden. Awaken, awaken, oh heralds of Spring."

Your incense is now blessed and consecrated for magical use. Burn it during all springtime rituals and magical workings. Close your circle as before.

SUMMER

S ummer celebrations begin at Beltaine, which is the third Wiccan fertility festival. Beltaine begins at sunset the evening before May 1 and lasts until sunset on May 1. The celebrations peak at the summer solstice before slowly fading into the fall colors of the harvest months. We are at the time of year when fresh, new green life is bursting out across the fields. We can now celebrate the growing time—the fertile and spirited time—that is filled to brimming with a summer's promise. Keywords are *fertility, abundance, magic, growth and advancement, love, celebration,* and *union/partings.*

Making a wand

When making a wand, you can shape it decoratively or keep it as plain as you wish. Since it will be your Fire Element tool, it should ideally be harvested from a living tree around midday on a dry, sunny day.

Summer correspondences

Red, orange, gold, oak leaves, the lion/lioness, frankincense, hawthorn, ivy, marigolds, rosemary, bergamot, green/gold candles.

Direction—South
Magical Tool—Wand
Time of Day—Midday

Observe which branch seems to be offered to you for your wand from the tree you have chosen. Consider oak or ash wood for making your wand, because these are Fire Element trees. However, this does not preclude you from using another species, should you or Nature wish.

❶ Take time to search out the tree that seems to wish to offer you some of its wood. Leave a handful of tobacco, which is a Fire Element herb

and speak to the tree spirit of your need and intentions before you harvest your wood. Wait for a feeling of rightness, a rustling of leaves, or a bird call that means you have been given permission.

❷ Cut your wood. (Your wand can be up to 18 inches (46 cm) in length.) Then cut out strips from the bark at this point, if you wish, while the branch is still fresh. Neaten the ends and leave your wand in a sacred place for a few days to dry out a little. Carve, whittle, and decorate with crystals, feathers, and other icons if you wish.

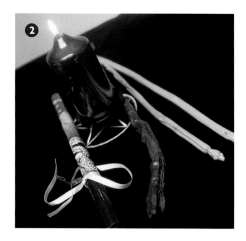

❸ Set up your altar in the South of your circle, the Fire Element direction on the wheel, with Summer's correspondences. Also add two green candles, one gold pillar candle, frankincense incense, a chalice of water, and a small bowl of salt. Then place your wand in the center beneath your gold candle. Open your circle.

❹ Consecrate your wand by following these steps:

1. Pass your wand through the incense smoke and say: "*By the powers of Air, be now cleansed and blessed.*"

2. Sprinkle the wand with water and say: "*By the powers of Water be now cleansed and blessed.*"

3. Sprinkle it with grains of salt and say: "*By the powers of Earth be now cleansed and blessed.*"

4. Pass the wand through the flame of the golden candle and say: "*By the powers of Fire, be now cleansed and blessed.*"

5. Hold your wand up to the South, and say: "*Lords of the eternal sun, enter now this wand of Fire, bring to life the flames of light to fill this wand with good and right. So mote it be.*"

6. Close your circle.

FALL

As fall approaches, the crops must be gathered and the harvest brought safely in before the weather changes. We have celebrated the first of three Wiccan harvest festivals—Lughnasadh (July 31)—as we approach the second harvest festival—Mabon— Fall equinox on the West of the Wiccan wheel, the direction of Water. Keywords are *healing, cleansing, love, relationships, female issues, emotions, sleep*, and *psychism*. Now is the time to seek balance in health, heart, and home. Repair, prepare for winter, and then celebrate the gifts of your year.

Making healing oils

In making fall healing oils, we are honoring the West's affinity with Water's healing powers. Oils for many purposes can be made throughout the year from seasonal vegetation using the same techniques.

Be aware of poisonous or toxic species and do not make up oils without proper care and attention to their properties. Please don't substitute healing oils for proper medical care. Do not use if you are pregnant.

Fall correspondences

Orange, ochre, brown, cassia bark, berries, fish, stag, grains, oats, apples, ears of corn, cornucopia, meadowsweet, myrtle.

Direction—West
Magical Tool—Chalice
Time of Day—Sunset

Wounded heart healing oil

The seasonal correspondences presented on this page are for Fall rituals and festivals. When working with healing, we need to look at correspondences for the planet of healing—

the moon. Since this wounded heart healing oil is used to alleviate relationship pains, we can also incorporate correspondences for the planet of love—Venus. Both are associated with the West. For this oil, you should set up your altar with Lunar and Venusian correspondences (see page 51).

❶ Gather your ingredients on or around the Fall equinox on a dry sunny day. Make absolutely sure that each flower head and the small twigs you pick are free from diseases and pests. Gather in a muslin bag to prevent bruising or damage.

- small apple wood branches
- 10 fl oz (300 ml) sweet almond oil
- ½ oz (15 g) chamomile flower heads
- ½ oz (15 g) daisy flower heads
- 5 drops palmarosa oil
- a handful of myrtle flowers (optional)
- jar or bottle and top

❷ Take your ingredients to your healing altar (orient the altar to the Western quarter of your working circle, with Venusian and Lunar representations) and lay them in the center. Light your altar candles and invoke the goddess

of love into your herbs by saying with your chalice over them:

"Queen of all hearts, a healing oil I make
From the meadows of your love; do not my
* heart forsake.*
Be with me Lady now; send your mystic Grace
Awaken my reflection in the beauty of love's face."

❸ Place your almond oil in the container and add your flower heads (see above). Seal the lid and shake gently. Close your circle. Leave on a warm windowsill for seven days, shaking every day. Strain through clean muslin until the fluid is clear. Add your palmarosa oil and shake again. Your oil is now ready to use. Anoint your heart and breast area before love rituals.

WINTER

The three harvest festivals have passed. Samhain (October 31) has been and gone, marking the turn of the Celtic year. Now we approach yule and the winter solstice in the North, the place of Winter on the Wiccan Wheel. Cold, bleak days—and even colder nights—cause us to withdraw, rest, and snuggle in the warmth. This is the time of year to make, weave, and create, as well as to meditate and visualize what you might wish to achieve in the year to come. Keywords are *wisdom, insight, envisioning, rest, renewal, material concerns, making crafts,* and *quality of life.* In crafting something during the winter months, we are emulating the customs of our pagan ancestors.

Crafting an altar cloth
You can put any design on your cloth, either in a central position or on one or all corners, depending upon your preferences.

Winter correspondences
Black, white, olive green, the pentagram, cauldron, owl, raven, bat, cypress, evergreens, pine aromatherapy oil.

Direction—North
Magical Tool—Pentagram
Time of Day—Midnight

❶ Decide what you are going to use for your altar. Then measure its dimensions. Use a dressmaker's tape measure to determine the size of your altar because its flexibility will enable you to bend around and along the surfaces accurately. Decide how much material you would like to hang down at the sides and measure up, over, and down from these points. Add an extra inch (2.5 cm) all the way around for hemming.

❷ Your altar cloth can be any color, so you need to select a favored color scheme. Most Wiccan altars are covered with a black cloth (usually with a silver or white design, when one is used). Hem the cloth and mark the center of your material with tailor's chalk.

❸ Using chalk, draw around a large plate laid on the center of your cloth. Draw your pentagram design inside this circle, again using the chalk (any line errors you make will wash out easily). With either threads or fabric paints in your choice of colors, etch in the lines of your design and leave to dry.

❹ Lay out your altar in the North with Winter correspondences, incense, a bowl of salt, a bowl of spring water, and two white altar candles. Then lay your folded altar cloth in the center. At midnight, open your circle.

3

5 Consecrate your cloth by following these steps:

1. Pass your cloth through the incense smoke and say: "*By the powers of Air, be now cleansed and blessed.*"

2. Pass your cloth above the flame of the candle and say: "*By the powers of Fire, be now cleansed and blessed.*"

3. Sprinkle it with water and say: "*By the powers of Water, be now cleansed and blessed.*"

4. Sprinkle it with grains of salt and say: "*By the powers of Earth, be now cleansed and blessed.*"

5. Hold your cloth up to the North and say: "*Lady white, on wings of night bestow this cloth with good and right. So mote it be!*"

Your cloth is now consecrated for use. Close your circle.

CHAPTER 6

DIVINATION AND WICCAN SKILLS

"Darksome night and shining moon
Hearken to the witches' rune.
East then South, West then North
Hear! Come! I call thee forth."

THE WITCHES' RUNE

When we are able to make profound connections with nature and with the powers of Creation—through dedication, devotion, and service to them—we, in turn, receive their blessings of clarity, intuition, and increased perception. This is because our eyes have been opened to more than the intellectual or the physical alone. Anyone can develop divination skills if they learn how to listen, how to feel, and how to act appropriately. Some will find this easier to achieve than others. You may have more natural empathy with crystals or healing, or the more practical aspects of Wicca instead. Whatever your skills, you should trust and develop your natural abilities without anxiety about those that don't come so easily to you. They will come in time.

Divination skills are like muscles. The more you use them, the more flexible and strong they grow to be. Just like anything in life, the more you familiarize yourself with something the more trustworthy it becomes. When someone first starts out reading palms or tarot cards, for example, they may well miss certain things. With practice, understanding, and experience, they can become adept at their chosen skill.

In this chapter we explore spell casting, charms, the witch's ladder, candle magic, and banishings. Wiccan magical skills require practice and understanding before they can work at full power. It is our will, and our mental focus, and the ability to conjure or feel the feelings associated with our magical intent that make Wiccan magic what it is. Developing willpower, concentration, and feelings are paramount to understanding Wiccan divination skills.

SPELL CASTING

To spell was magic! In days of old the common people could not read or write. To see runic or ogham symbols (ogham is the Druid's sacred magical alphabet) carved into a rock or a staff covered in coded language was an incredible ability. This was especially powerful because these "talking" symbols could be left anywhere by someone who had long departed. It was seen as a magical ability to be able to write using these (and other) magical alphabets. Therefore, when symbols were put together to create a spell or charm, they were like pure magic flowing from the gods. Our verb "to spell" originates from the same source. To be able to spell out your magic was considered miraculous. Any witches, shamans, heathens, or pagans with this ability were treated with very high regard!

Many people have reservations about spell casting and there is very good reason for this. We live in a dimension where what we ask for is provided, exactly as we ask for it. We are co-creators with our universe and as such can rise to meet Spirit halfway with any request that is potentially possible on our destiny path. I may well want to sing on stage, but if I am tone deaf I am deluding myself and should be more realistic about my talents and abilities. If I ask for millions of dollars, I am being greedy and missing the point. The best form of spell casting is the kind that calls for personal improvements such as greater courage, deeper love, or healing for others. In other words, "unconditional magic" is the best form to practice. Most of us begin the magical path by casting spells, creating charms, and weaving magic purely for the purpose of improving our own lives

in some way. As we progress along the Wiccan path, our magic becomes more and more altruistic and unconditional. By the advanced stages, we tend to cast very few, if any, personal spells.

Spell casting requires planning, timing, ingredients, and focus. The first step is to plan

Ogham symbols, derived from the ancient magical druidic alphabet, carved into a standing stone in Eire.

what your spell is to be about. Then you need to discover the most appropriate time to cast your chosen spell. Your schedule needs to allow you time to gather your ingredients.

Finally, when you are ready to cast your spell, you need to focus your willpower within a ritual. This may seem simple, but you should take an adequate amount of time to plan your spell because your words must be very precise. To say, "I need a break from work" will bring you the "need" for a break. To say, "I want a new car" will bring you all the requirements for a new car but

very likely leave you "wanting" for an actual vehicle! Be careful how you wish and read your words very carefully. Take plenty of time to "spell" out your spells correctly!

Never manipulate the free will of others nor harm anyone else through your magic. Maintain dignity and integrity at all times and remember your Oath that you will not intentionally harm others in any way. Work for the highest good, consider your real needs, and remember to give back as well as take from universal goodwill by being of service to others.

THE RHYMING COUPLET

T he simplest and often the most effective form of spell casting is known as "the rhyming couplet." This is a two-line chant that has been specifically created to express poetically the spell required. The rhyming couplet is absorbed more easily by our subconscious, which is the place within us where magic percolates and is formed. This is because our subconscious responds to symbols, hypnotic repetition, and those feelings beyond everyday language that can be accessed more readily by the use of poetry.

The spell that follows can be adapted to suit any requirement simply by making up your own two-line rhymes.

The rhyming couplet can be performed with any form of magic (such as while making a charm, talisman, witch's ladder, or healing poppet [doll-like representation of a person], or casting a spell). It acts like the punctuation that directs the focus of your spell toward its desired result. The best form of rhyme is one that expresses the desired result as if it had already happened.

To make a herbal spell charm

❶ Consider what you are trying to achieve and then compose a two-line poem, for example, "*Ruby's leg is healed of pain, she can now walk well again*," or "*Sally's heart was filled with tears, now love and joy replace her fears.*"

❷ Purchase about 18 inches (46 cm) of organza, voile, or loose muslin, and about one yard (one meter) of appropriately colored ribbon for your spell's focus (such as purple for luck or pink for love). Gather the required herbs and floral fragrances, as well as a small crystal.

❸ Set up your altar in the North or appropriate elemental direction from the spell chart, laid out with appropriate herbal, crystal, and floral correspondences for your particular spell (see table opposite). Open your circle.

❹ All the time you are making your spell charm, repeat your rhyme quietly under your breath. Cut two five-inch (13-cm) squares out of organza or loosely woven muslin. Hem them together around three edges, leaving one side open. Fill with your herbs, oils, crystals, and/or flowers. Sew up. Decorate the edges with the ribbon as you wish. Close your circle.

TABLE OF CORRESPONDENCES FOR SPELLS

SPELL	LOVE	WEALTH	FRIENDSHIP	SUCCESS	HEALING	PROTECTION (The Pentagram)	LUCK
COLOR	green/pink	green	green	gold/orange	blue	red	turquoise/purple/lilac
GEM	emerald	ruby	golden topaz	amber	pearl	jet	star sapphire
CRYSTAL	rose quartz	citrine	malachite/jade	sunstone	moonstone	obsidian/smoky quartz	turquoise
ELEMENT	Water	Fire/Earth	Water	Fire	Water	Fire/Earth	Fire/Earth
DAY OF WEEK	Friday	Thursday	Friday	Sunday	Monday	Tuesday	Thursday
PLANET	Venus	Jupiter	Venus	Sun	Moon	Mars	Jupiter
HERB	myrtle	cloves	love-in-a-mist	cinnamon/frankincense	sandalwood/camphor	cayenne pepper/garlic	cinquefoil/nutmeg
FLOWER	rose	marigold	sweet pea	sunflower	lily	garlic	heather
TREE	apple	almond/horse chestnut	plum	bay	eucalyptus	holly/pine needles	oak
DEITY	Aphrodite/Venus Branwen	Lakshmi Juno Pan	Janus	Apollo	Bridget Isis	choice of Hecate or Cerridwen or Anubis	Jupiter The Dagda
METAL	copper	gold	copper	gold	silver	iron	copper/tin
DIRECTION	West	North	West	South	West	North	North
SIGIL	♡	∿	♡	✝	♄	∿	∿

A SPELL FOR GOOD LUCK

We need to remember that whenever we are casting or creating spells, they will be answered in some way by the universe. This means that whenever we ask for anything such as success, we should prepare to have the limits or barriers to that success revealed to us in our lives. If we call for wealth, then we must prepare to be shown what needs to be cleared away in order for that wealth to arrive. This is called meeting your spell halfway, which is always a requirement in magic. You cannot expect a sweeping result with little or no effort or openness on your part. This is why magical practitioners and witches alike are always very careful before spell-weaving. They know the meaning of calling for something to change, and the work and effort that may well be necessary to bring about the desired results. Remember, too, that when you call for something you know is not yours you are forsaking your magical oath, which will backfire on you at some point!

This spell for good luck can be worn as a necklace, hung somewhere privately, carried in a pocket or draped on your bed.

Hag stones or goddess stones are well-known protectors and averters of misfortune. Although most commonly found on beaches, they can be found when walking anywhere. If you wish to make this good luck necklace, ask the Goddess to help you find a suitable stone, or to lead you to where you can find one.

❶ Find a stone with a hole through the center, which is called a "holey stone" or "hag stone," and choose turquoise and/or black beads, and little copper and white metal findings. Purchase about one yard (one meter) of thin black necklace cord.

❷ Set up your altar in the center of your circle with the correspondences you have chosen from the chart, associated with a spell for good luck (see page 87). Lay out your necklace ingredients in the center of your altar. Open your circle in the usual way.

❸ Repeat the chant with your athame over your ingredients:

"Lady, mother, sister, lover,
Goddess, crone, and bride.
This I make for love of You
Let good luck here reside."

Make your necklace by threading the looped thread through the hole and passing the two ends through the loop to secure the stone to the cord.

Thread your two ends through your chosen beads, repeating your chant to the goddess as you go, until completed. Knot the two ends together to finish your good luck necklace.

❹ Bless your necklace with the four Elemental tools of incense, candle flame, water, and salt and then close your circle.

A HEALING SPELL IN MERLIN'S SACRED GROVE

H ealing spells, like all spells, can be many and varied. This particular spell works with the magical powers of Merlin, the great Celtic sorcerer and devotee of the Goddess, from whom he learned all about herbs, healing, and the wilds of nature. He is a master of herb lore and healing as well as being an honorable protector, counselor, and occult guide. For this spell you will ideally need a bent silver coin. To bend a coin you will need to hammer it. This represents "killing" the coin thus freeing it into Spirit with your wish.

This healing spell is called a visualization, a mental journey in this instance to Merlin. Rather than making a material object, you will be working with the powers of your mind, which is just as valid in magic as making an item you can physically see. Use a full or waning moon for this ritual.

Sacred music can be played if you wish.

❶ Set up your altar in the center of the circle, with olive green candles, a bent silver coin, and a small bowl of spring water. If you have one, include a statue of the Goddess or a picture you have chosen to represent her, decked in nature's finery and greenery, so that your altar is abundant with the goddess's beauty. Set up cushions or a comfortable chair in front of your altar and then cast your sacred circle.

❷ Perform the Fourfold Breath and then sit or lie down. Play back your recording or begin your journey to Merlin's Sacred Grove now.

Imagine that you are standing in the center of an ancient circle of majestic oak trees. There is a

sacred well in the center. You carry a small bent silver coin in your hand. You can see that this is a truly sacred and magical grove, a clearing where the worlds can meet and merge. There is an atmosphere of mystical peace. The air is pure, the colors rich, and the waters in the well are cool and clear. You look around the circle of trees and notice that before each one stands a healing being and that emerging from the shadows, beyond the grove, is a commanding presence, with flowing robes and a staff inscribed with magical symbols, topped with a large crystal ball, held in the sculpted claws of a spirit dragon. This is Merlin. You greet each other and move together by the well. He stirs the waters with his staff to call forth the healing maiden of the well. She rises on a cloud of stars and the finest mist you ever did see. Speak your healing wish to her and throw the bent silver coin respectfully into her sacred well.

Give your thanks, listen to any words that may be spoken there, and then bid her and Merlin farewell. Bow to the beings, to the trees, to the Grove, and leave, returning gradually to everyday consciousness.

❸ Recall your journey, reaffirm your wish, and then drop the coin on your altar into your water bowl. Close your circle and leave your bowl and coin under the full moon for three nights. Give this coin to whomever the spell was for. Honor any help you receive by loving the Earth.

❷

A SPELL FOR LOVE

The art of finding true love is a noble quest and one that most of us hope will be gifted to us in our lifetime. Many people have experienced broken relationships. Very few have experienced the beauty of lasting love. When we look at the reasons for this, it is often because we enter relationships still carrying the wounds and bruises from our previous ones and so are unconsciously attracted to individuals who will trigger events that will show us these wounds. Hence their failure, for very few of us choose to work on ourselves, preferring instead to blame the other for any relationship shortcomings.

❶ Healing the wounds

In order for magic to work, we must rise to meet it, doing what we can to prepare the way. This spell is aimed at healing the heart, then preparing for love and finally to calling openly for your beloved.

Ingredients:

- 1 rose quartz crystal hand chosen by you
- 7 drops rose geranium essential oil
- 3½ fl oz (100 ml) pure sesame oil
- 3½ fl oz (100 ml) dropper bottle (available from pharmacies)

The apple tree is one of the trees of love. Apple blossom can signify a new love affair.

On a Friday evening just after the full moon, place ingredients on your West-facing altar laid out in pinks and greens, with your chalice, any love icons, and a Venus or love deity statue if you have one. Music can be played. Light your two pink altar candles and open your circle as usual. Dedicate your ingredients to healing the heart by holding your chalice over your ingredients saying:

Chalice invocation:
"Awaken now spirits of healing
Awaken now calming all fear,
Heal the wounds in my heart my Lady
that love may enter here."

Add seven drops of rose geranium oil to your sesame oil. Anoint yourself and then pick up your crystal, and smooth it with the oil mix while thinking of your feelings, and past relationships. Ask the crystal to help you heal any wounds. Close your circle and then bury your crystal in the ground, either beneath an apple tree or with one-half of an apple cut lengthwise.

❷ Preparing for love

On a Friday, during the waxing (increasing) moon, set up your altar as before using a chrysocolla crystal and palmarosa oil instead of rose quartz and rose geranium oil. Follow the Step One instructions while considering what kind of partner you would like. Put the crystal under your pillow.

Chalice Invocation:
"Awaken now spirits
of healing
Awaken now drawing
love near
Open my heart my Lady
that love may enter here."

❸ Calling your beloved

On a Friday night during a full moon, lay out your altar as before, this time with a ruby and orris root powder. Work as before, but this time visualize your lover coming to you.

Chalice Invocation:
"My heart is open
no longer broken
Lover now come to me."

Carry this crystal with you until love arrives.

RUNES

The Runes are a symbolic alphabet that form part of the Northern European magical tradition. Scandinavian legend tells of the Norse God Odin bringing them to Midgard (the human world) by hanging from Yggdrasil (The World Tree). They are both powerful and uncompromising in their message. The word rune means "secret" or "mystery," and each one carries a specific message linked to the mysteries of Creation. Linked also with the Norns, or three sisters of fate—Skuld (birth), Verdhandi (life), and Urd (death)—the runes can help and guide us toward making the right decisions and choices in order to fulfill our greatest potential and thus meet our truest destiny (for the Runic alphabet, see opposite).

Creating a magical signature

You can transcribe your name into runic symbols by replacing the letters of your name with their equivalent runes. This can then be used as your "magical signature" on wands, talismans, written wishes, or spell bags, for example.

❶ Exchange the letters of your chosen name onto a piece of draft paper. Sally, for example, would become ᚴ ᚠ ᚱ ᚱ ᚼ, the runes for regeneration, inspiration, the flow of feelings, and gradual success. This is the basis of your magical signature and can be used as is.

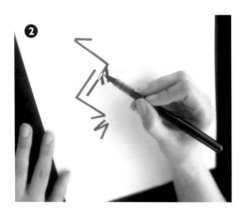

❷ You can create different designs and arrange your runic letters if you like to make an artistic pattern or magical shield of your name. The example I have designed here from the letters for Sally is actually very apt because it is snakelike; a creature I am closely connected to in my own magical work.

❸ If you have designed something for magical use (a shield, pattern, wand, or talisman) using your runic signature on it, it should be consecrated in a sacred circle with the four Elements if you wish to activate it (see page 19).

Making a bind rune

A bind rune is a design made up of two or more runic symbols, traditionally used by Norse warriors as tokens of power. Design your own combinations or make your own "successful partnerships" bind rune by combining the "F" rune with the "G" rune into symmetrically balanced shapes as shown here.

RUNES AND THEIR MEANINGS

LETTER	SIGN	MEANING	LETTER	SIGN	MEANING
A	ᚠ	Inspiration	N	ᚼ	Patience
B	ᛒ	Fruitfulness	O	ᛜ	Parting
C	ᚲ	Clarity	P	ᛍ	Choices, the inner child
D	ᛞ	Transformation	Q	ᚲ	(use "C" rune)
E	ᛖ	Assimilation	R	ᚱ	Life direction
F	ᚦ	Accomplishment	S	ᛋ	Regeneration
G	ᚷ	Partnerships	T	↑	Conquest
H	ᚺ	Tests and challenges	U	ᚢ	Inner strength
I	ᛁ	Suspension	V	ᚢ ᚹ	(Choose either)
J	ᛇ	Gradual success	W	ᚹ	Joyfulness
K	ᚲ	(use "C" Rune)	X	ᚲᛋ	(Used together)
L	ᛚ	The flow of feelings & emotions	Y	ᛇ	Gradual success
M	ᛗ	Assimilation	Z	ᛉ	Protection

DIVINATION AND WICCAN SKILLS

THE WITCH'S LADDER

The Witch's Ladder probably first originated as an aid to concentration and spell chanting because it is traditionally a length of rope with forty knots or beads along its length, much like a string of religious prayer beads. It would, therefore, have served the purpose of allowing the witch to lose herself in her activity without having to count the number of chants as well.

The Witch's Ladder we will be making here is a very personal charm and one that should be made in a sacred manner, preferably upon a Sabbat or important date in your calendar, like your birthday.

On the night of any full moon, affirm to Lady Luna that you wish to make a witch's ladder and would like to be guided to your nine feathers. Over a period of time, gradually gather these nine feathers from the wild as you find them. They can be any size or color and from any bird. Once this task is completed, no matter how long it takes, you can move into the next phase. Purchase three thin cords, each five feet (150 cm) in length, in colors that best describe your spiritual potential. If, for example, you wish to be loving, creative, and wise, you could use pink, orange, and black together. For a ladder associated with the Triple Goddess, use black (crone), white (maiden), and red (mother) cords.

❶ On your chosen special night, set up your altar in the North, with your ladder ingredients laid out in the center of the altar. Include your four consecration items (see page 19).

❷ Consecrate your ingredients with the four Elements (page 19) before commencing making your ladder. Once this is done, knot the three cords at one end and begin plaiting them together.

❸ Continue until you reach the other end of the cords, leaving about a five-inch (13-cm) space between the plaited part and where you will secure your second knot. This is the space where you will add your feathers.

CORRESPONDENCES FOR CORD COLORS

RED	ORANGE	YELLOW	GREEN	BLUE	PURPLE	VIOLET	BLACK	WHITE	PINK
Fire	Fire	Air	Earth	Water	Fire/Earth	Fire/Air	Earth	Earth	Fire
courage	creativity	communication	harmony	healing	inner richness	spirituality	wisdom	purity	love

❹ Gather your feathers up and put the ends through your space crosswise and then tie your second knot around them to secure them in place.

Bless by holding up to the North and saying:

"Cords of three, and feathers nine
this charm shall my good fortune find
and to itself all mischief bind.
My Lady, Lord be here entwined."

Option two

As an aid to concentration and spell chanting, sacredly make your witch's ladder with one five-foot (150-cm) length of black cord, strung with either forty beads or secured with forty knots along its length, moving along it one bead/knot at a time, when you are chanting.

CANDLE MAGIC

Candles are a vital part of rituals and magic. They also signify the Fire Element and its spiritual qualities of transformation, illumination, and protection. Because of the flame and what it symbolizes, candle magic is transformative, revealing, and protective. It is always possible to change a situation or mood simply by lighting a candle. You can light candles for others too. Remember to repeat "An it be for highest good and by Divine Will …" to ensure the wisest outcome.

To anoint an appropriately colored candle with specific herbs, flowers, spices, or oils is to enhance and give potency to the effectiveness of your candle magic, the Fire Element, and the qualities you wish to invoke. Again, we move back to studying pertinent correspondences for our chosen magical focus.

CANDLE CORRESPONDENCES

PURPOSE	Prosperity, material matters, employment	Travel, calling for change, moving home, or work	Courage, health energy, passion, protection	Healing, emotional peace, harmony in relationships	Pure Love, spiritual peace, grace, blessings
ELEMENT	Earth	Air	Fire	Water	Spirit
CANDLE COLOR	olive green	sunshine yellow	red/orange	blue	white
PLANT	fern	clover/bamboo	bergamot	jasmine	white lily
HERB	sage	peppermint	basil	vervain	lotus root
OIL	vetivert	lavender	frankincense	sandalwood	rose
SPICE	salt	anise	cinnamon	coconut	saffron

Candle anointing

Refer to the table opposite to find the column that most closely suits your focus. If you are seeking spiritual peace, for example, your candle color would be white. Looking down the column, you then need to decide whether to anoint your candle with fresh flowers, herbs, an essential oil, or a spice (in the case of spiritual peace, saffron). When using oils, try to obtain an essence that is natural rather than synthetic. Other correspondences can be displayed on the altar if you wish, such as a vase of white roses when working with Spirit.

❶ Prepare your room and yourself. Set up your altar with your candle and anointing ingredient, and a small bowl to contain it in the center. Open your circle in the usual way.

❷ Hold your pillar candle in your dominant hand (which means your writing hand) and beginning at the center of the candle's body, rub the chosen flower, herb, oil, or spice from the center to the top and then from the center downward, until the candle is fully dressed.

❸ As you are anointing your candle, you can also repeat a rhyming couplet, made up to encapsulate the focus of your magic, whispering it under your breath in a hypnotic repetitive way (such as "Moving on, moving on, trials and tribulations gone").

❹ Dedicate your candle to its magical intent by saying the following when you have anointed and ignited it:

"*Spirit of this Sacred Flame*
By all that's hallowed in thy name,
I invoke thee—I invoke thee
Enter now and light the way
to [state your magical intent here,
such as a loving heart or peace]."

❺ Close your circle. You can light your anointed pillar candle every time you wish to reaffirm its magic for as long as you wish. (Please don't leave naked flames unattended.)

BANISHINGS

L ife has two aspects: dark and light, night and day, happy and sad, good and evil. This is the nature of our duality—its purpose is to help us find balance and harmony within these polar opposites and, with this in mind, we now look at banishing. In order to know light, we must have darkness. In order to attain enlightenment we must, therefore, understand the shadow-lands. The shadow-lands are those aspects of ourselves that are unexplored, unrealized, trapped, or manipulated by ignorance (such as habitual emotional reactions, stealing, or self-abuse).

Energy is everywhere, both in the shadows and the light of our being. To banish something is to command its removal. If we banish unwanted emotional or psychic energy, we should also remember to fill that space afterward with symbols or qualities of light.

This banishing can be performed to clear an environment before undertaking rituals, or to remove unwanted or excess emotional or psychic energy.

❶ Make a small portable altar if you need to clear more than one area. Set up your altar with one large white altar candle and one slightly smaller black candle in the center of your area, then add a bell.

❷ You will need a pestle and mortar, two bowls, and a heatproof container (such as a scallop shell) and your athame. Measure out your dried exorcism blend ingredients (see below) into one of your bowls. Blend and grind them down to small pieces, little by little, in your pestle and mortar, placing your blended ingredients into another bowl for the time being.

Ingredients:
2 parts frankincense
1 part copal
1 part yarrow
1 part angelica leaves
8 drops rosemary essential oil

❸ Once this is completed, add your rosemary oil and mix together thoroughly. Place a large pinch of your mix into your heatproof container on top of burning charcoal. (Please beware—the container will get very hot underneath.) Light your black candle.

❹ Walk from the area entrance in a counter-clockwise direction, wafting your herbs into every corner, window, doorway, and opening until you are back at the entrance. Pick up your black candle and walk again around the room in a counter-clockwise direction, doing a banishing pentagram in each corner as you say:

*"Begone oh shadows, fiends of night
Phantoms, demons now take flight."*

Put your black candle back on the altar and extinguish it.

5 Light your white candle and walk clockwise around the room saying:

*"All in turmoil be at peace
By light of Spirit, now released."*

6 Put your white candle back on the altar while it is still burning and pick up your bell. Ring the bell toward all directions as you turn from the altar. Thank Spirit and extinguish your white candle.

This process can be repeated in every room of your house, office, or building in case you want to cleanse your entire building rather than just a single room.

A WICCAN BANISHING RITUAL

High Magic includes a ritual called the Lesser Banishing Ritual of the Pentagram, which is highly effective in removing unwanted influences from environments. It works with the powers of the pentagram (the five-pointed star) to banish from Earth to Spirit in a continuous movement around the star until you reach where you first started. This can be done with pointed fingers. Or, if you can manage the movements, you can hold a magical tool such as your athame or wand. Use it prior to magical work and to cleanse environments.

The ritual has been adapted here to correspond with Wiccan deities rather than with the traditional Judeo-Christian archetypes used by high magicians. This does not make it any less effective as a banishing tool.

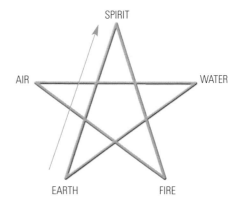

❶ Visualize a shimmering, silver pentagram shining brightly in the heavens. Let the star descend into your crown down to your brow. Put your palms together, touch the center of your brow, and say:

"Thou who art the beauty of moon and stars."

❷ Visualize the star moving into your heart, then take both your hands down to the heart and say:

"And the Sacred heart of all kindness."

❸ Now visualize the star going down into your stomach, still shining brightly. Place one hand palm down on either side of your stomach and say:

"And the mother of all things."

When performing a Banishing Pentagram, begin in the lower left-hand corner moving upward and complete the star in one continuous movement.

❹ Let the star come back up to the heart, where it expands and radiates silver light throughout your whole being. Bring your hands back up to the heart, place them one over the other, and say:

"And the light within my spirit."

❺ Remain silent for a while until you are filled with our Lady's light. Then imagine as you open your hands from the heart outward before you, with your palms uppermost, that the light is now radiating into the world and extending all around you. Then say:

"Descend upon me now and heed my call."

❻ Face East and draw a flaming silver banishing pentagram in the air with your fingers or athame and say, "*Athene.*" Draw an imaginary line along the ground from the Eastern star until you reach South. Do as before and say, "*Astarte.*" Move West, repeat the pentagram and say, "*Hecate.*" Move North, repeat, and say: "*The Eumenedes*". Complete the circle back to East.

❼ Raise your athame/fingers to the heavens and then down to the East again and say:

"*Before me Artemis.*"

❽ Raise your arm over your head and point backwards saying:

"*Behind me, Nepthys.*"

❾ Bring your arm back over to your right saying: "*To my right, Anatu.*"

❿ Point or pass your athame to your left saying:

"*To my left, The Morrigu.*"

⓫ Bring your arms to your heart, palms together, pause a moment and then say:

"*Above me shines the Goddess, about me and within me shines her radiant star.*"

Your banishing ritual is now complete.

CHAPTER 7

INNER JOURNEYS

"All that is gold does not glitter
Not all those who wander are lost.
The old that is strong does not weaken
Deep roots are not reached by the frost."

THE SONG OF ARAGORN, J.R.R. TOLKIEN

E very step we take—every choice we make—is part of our life's outward journey. Inner journeys, on the other hand, are those taken to our spirit and to our soul. They represent our inner world rather than our outer one. Human beings have throughout history ignored the message of the wise ones given to us time and time again. That message is: "that which we seek is found within." This simple truth is hard to grasp even when we are not in the throes of confusion or chaos. Nonetheless it is the truth. All answers to every single one of our dilemmas or questions lie within us. It is just a question of knowing how to access the inner world.

This chapter gives you information on finding your animal familiar, the basics of astral travel, and suggestions for creating your own journeys. These give opportunities to explore your inner world and build a relationship to it.

Keywords to connecting with your inner world include trust, faith, and commitment. Trust that the messages you receive may well contain truth. Have faith that what you need will find you and answer you, and develop commitment to inner world practices so that you regularly devote a certain amount of time to your spiritual self.

At first you may find it hard to trust the messages from your inner world. Test any answers or guidance you receive if you like. If they are true, they will remain so. The more you utilize your perceptions, the easier their language becomes to understand. With time, you will begin to trust yourself so completely that you will come to know that you really are your very best teacher and friend.

FAMILIARS

I define *familiars* as animal helpers or spiritual allies that are intimately linked to the Wiccan practitioner by their "familiarity." A familiar can be a physical creature that actually lives under the same roof, but can also be a spirit presence. The main functions of a familiar are to guard, guide, and inform as well as to share their qualities in a deeply magical and spiritual way. Pets can sometimes be our familiars, if we feel an especially profound connection with them. The most important factor about your familiar is that their innate qualities will also be part of your character that you either develop or work with, such as dog (loyalty, guardianship, and love) or cat (psychic understanding, awareness, and perception).

You can call upon the powers of your familiar as you need or want to and also learn a great deal from them. Consider other animals' powers such as hawk for clarity or ant for teamwork. If you respect nature all life will respond to you and cooperate with you too.

To find your familiar

❶ Set up your altar with dried herbs of horehound in the East, dragon's blood powder in the South, catnip in the West, and coltsfoot in the North, with a white candle set in the center. Cast your circle.

❷ Light your white candle. Take a pinch of horehound and cast it into the white candle flame, saying: *"Air of Spirit, by air you may come, if you be a wingèd one."*
Take a pinch of dragon's blood powder and say, *"Fire of Spirit, by Fire you may come, if you be of golden sun."*
Take a pinch of catnip and cast it into the white candle and say, *"Water of Spirit, by Water you may*

come, if by silver moon you're spun."
Cast your coltsfoot into the candle and say, *"Earth of Spirit, by Earth you may come, if you be from Earthly home."*
Face each of the four directions and ring a bell toward the four quarters.

❸ Lie down or sit in a comfortable chair and begin your journey. If you have difficulty remembering, you may choose to record the words before you start and play them back while you take the journey.

You find yourself standing in an ethereal temple that is shimmering and mysterious. There is a fountain in the center. Before you stand Pan and Gaia. Pan the goat-footed god is playing a haunting melody on his pipes. Gaia, the Goddess of our Earth, sits upon a bower decked in flowers, greenery, and oak-moss. You kneel before them and speak your request to find your familiar. Wait respectfully. You then hear sounds. As you look around, you see a creature approaching the Lady

and Lord by water or air, or on foot. They speak with it and guide it to you with their blessing. This is your spirit familiar in whatever form it has taken. Acknowledge your gift. Give thanks and then slowly come back to everyday consciousness.

❹ Close your circle and find something that represents your familiar to carry with you (such as a pendant, picture, or statue). Connect with your familiar whenever you wish.

ASTRAL TRAVEL

A stral travel involves making journeys beyond and apart from the physical body. With practice and experience, astral travel loosens the grip of the physical and mortal world upon the subtler energy within our psyche; our spirit. Astral travel should be treated as an aspect of, rather than as a replacement for, real life. It should never be used to spy upon or otherwise manipulate reality. Please use it only for the greater good. Not everyone feels comfortable with astral travel, finding it less easy to leave the security of a physical body. These people can still create an astral room and visit it simply as an inner sanctuary.

The astral room

An astral room is a magical place where you can go for sanctuary from worldly troubles for a while, or you can energetically launch yourself from it into the astral realms with faith and confidence.

Your astral room must be an extension of your character and represent who you believe you are. You must feel totally comfortable and safe there.

Begin by visualizing in your mind a room that is like an extension of yourself. You can include Elementals (such as a spirit guide, animals, birds, flowers, trees, and waterfalls). In fact, you can include anything that you wish; there are no limitations upon what you place in this room. It doesn't have to have four square walls. It could be circular or be bounded on all sides by tree roots or cave walls. What is important is that there is some kind of clearly defined boundary all the way around your space.

There should be one door through which you enter and leave. Another door that is opposite to the first is the one through which you step when taking and returning from an astral journey. These two doors should fit securely and be easy to open and close.

Your astral room is as real on the etheric level as a physical room is in the material world, and should be treated with equal belief. You are in control of your astral room. If you wanted to change it, you would visualize performing those tasks (such as decorating it, putting up a picture, or clearing away some leaves). You can visit your room at any time without journeying through the astral doorway. The more time you spend in your astral room, the more tangible it becomes until it represents a place of real safety and sanctuary.

Taking an astral journey

When taking an astral journey, enter your room through the first doorway. Prepare yourself for the journey as if you were going on a physical journey. Make your intention clear as to where you are traveling. If Egypt is your destination, stand by the astral doorway when you are ready and say, "*To Egypt.*" Open the astral door and you will find sand, pyramids, and other characteristics of a scene in Egypt in front of you. BEFORE you step through the doorway, you must perform the banishing pentagram of Earth to Spirit (see pages 102–103) to protect yourself. Once your journey is completed, return through the astral doorway to your room. Turn and face where you have been, and draw the banishing pentagram again to seal the door. Close it, unpack if you need to, and take time to arrive back in your astral room completely before stepping back through the other doorway to normal physical reality.

CREATING YOUR OWN JOURNEYS

E ach and every one of us will travel a life path that is unique. It may be very similar to the paths of others, but it is always colored by our own individual characters. Because of this, it is very helpful to know how to create our own spirit journeys. That way we can access inner knowing for guidance on any situation in our life, tailoring each journey to suit specific needs.

We are now going to establish the foundation for a psychic journey. We need to establish it, firmly and clearly, down to the finest detail in order to be able to define a "walk, ride, flight, or whatever mode of travel" in the imagination that remains constant in its detail. To give you an example, you may perhaps begin your journey by walking through a five-bar gate onto a path in a forest. There are fir trees to your left and a mountain in the distance. The sky is clear and blue. To your right is a rising hill covered in smaller trees. Nestled among these is a log cabin. This image would be your starting point and should always stay the same. Perhaps then your path

takes you down a slope toward a lake. You walk part way around the lake and sit on a bench. Then you stand up and continue to follow the path around the water's edge, back to your original pathway, and up the slope to the gate.

This psychic walk should become crystal clear in your mind, down to whether or not there is smoke coming out of the cabin chimney each time you enter the gate. Is the lake clear and large, or smaller and filled with reeds? Plan your route and stick to its original scenery every time you take this walk.

Perhaps you wish to discover why someone has betrayed you so that you can move on from the experience. The key word here is "betrayal" and so you can dedicate your next

"walk" to discovering why this happened. All you need to do is vocalize your intent to Spirit that you wish to receive information and guidance from them, and that you are going to take your psychic walk to find their spiritual message.

You should discover that, as you take your walk, things appear that are not normally there. Perhaps Pan is dancing on the path as you reach it or an old woman gathering sticks gives you a rune, or whatever. Anything appearing that is different from the original walk you created will be psychic information or a helpful spirit coming in to join you.

Thus you can create your own journeys, even down to, for example, having a temple by the lake in your original plan where someone may appear so you can have a conversation. Free your imagination and it will take you to the profound Wisdom of Ages held within your spirit, where truth can be found and understanding realized.

You can take your shamanic or psychic journeys outdoors too. Seek out special or magical areas in your local landscape as I have done over the years. I have named this waterfall in my village "Fairy Falls" because the spirit of the fae is powerful there.

INNER JOURNEYS

RITES AND RITUALS

"May the Circle be open, yet forever unbroken
May the love of the Goddess be forever in your heart.
Merry Meet and Merry Part and Merry Meet again."

TRADITIONAL WICCAN CHANT

Marking occasions in life is like providing punctuation to sentences. Without a form of acknowledgement, days can so easily run into each other and become dull, dry, and insignificant. To lift an experience into the wondrous—to offer initiation, advancement, and distinction—is to provide color, depth, and meaning to our progress through life. This is why Wiccans have rites of passage, and why they perform rituals and ceremonies. Life to us is colorful because we choose to pick up the paints of Creation and use them.

Rites of passage signify those times in our lives when we move from one phase to another. They can dignify our status so that as we leave one thing behind we are given acknowledgement that we are stepping into something else in its place. The occasions are given significance that, in turn, gives us a sense of meaning and validity as well. They can also be very helpful in defining the requirements of completion and closing before we step through the new door opening before us. By marking rites of passage, we move through life with a dignity and a purpose without too many threads of unfinished business left dangling behind us as we go.

Rituals serve the same purpose. They punctuate the years we live and bring connectedness and significance to our daily lives. They help us to honor occasions, to join the Wheel as it turns, and to celebrate its turning with joy and reverence. Rituals honor and respect the gifts of Creation, which are given so freely and unconditionally to us all.

MAGICAL NAMING

Magical names are an age-old tradition, ranging from the ancient priesthood to the pagan. Historically, they were sometimes used to keep real identities secret during times of religious persecution. Adopting a magical name sustains a magical identity and creates something "special" about you when you use it. It distinguishes between the mundane and magical worlds, especially if you use it only for "Craft" work. A magical name can be adopted by anyone (Wiccan or otherwise) to mark an initiation as a witch, to create a new image, or perhaps to denote a rite of passage. It chooses you, and is often evident all around you even if you don't realize it. It will either represent part of you or be something to which you can aspire. The name *Morningstar* ("the love that guides"), I try to emulate as best as I can!

Your magical name can change as you change and grow or it can remain with you for the whole of your life. If your name does seem to want to change, you can perform this ritual again and again to mark it as a rite of passage, fully acknowledged by a special event.

Names can come from anywhere (such as a deity, tree, flower, herb, mythical creature, elf, or fairy). They can also be combinations (such as Firespark or Moonhare). And let us not forget the simpler names such as Ember and Amber. Take time in accepting a name and ask for three signs from Spirit that this is indeed the name to which you are being guided.

Your name should appear in various ways around you. With the name Rowan, for example, you may be sent a postcard that pictures a rowan tree. Perhaps a gardening book falls open to the page describing rowan trees. Other indicators would include opportunities appearing in your life that require that name's qualities. In the case of Rowan, it would be magical guardianship and protection. These are the kind of signs that will appear. For detailed descriptions of name meanings, please consult reference books.

Once you have received your three signs, which can take any length of time, you can prepare for your naming ritual. You will need statuettes of a goddess and god and a veil.

Naming ritual

❶ Set up your altar to the North with icons of a goddess and god, and with two white candles. Open your circle. Stand before your altar, drop your veil over your face, and declare:

"O Mighty Lord and Gracious Lady, I stand before you to seek your blessings upon the name hereby bestowed upon me. Bear witness that I enter here in perfect love and perfect trust and from this day on I shall honor my name with love. Hearken; for I leave the everyday world behind (ring a bell and pause) *"and mark this moment with my magical name* [state magical name here]. *So mote it be."*

Then declare:

"By the powers of the Goddess and the great Horned God, I now step beyond the things of this world, free of worldly shackles (take a step toward your altar). Lift your veil and say *"and my eyes now see as the eyes of* [state your magical name here]."

"So mote it be."

❷ Kiss the back of each of your hands once. Ring a bell, and then close your circle in the usual way.

WICCAN RITES AND BLESSINGS

In these closing pages, you will find some Wiccan Rites and Blessings that include ceremonies for children, marriage, becoming an elder, and those times when a loved one dies. Nothing written here should be considered sacrosanct. If you would like to change any of the wording to suit your own requirements, please do feel free to do so.

These rituals can provide the blueprints for you to compose your own rituals and blessings as you grow in confidence and understanding. There is no difference between you and me except in experience. If I can write rituals, you can too!

The most important points to remember in rituals and rites of passage are the reasons for them, and the kind of structure you would like. It is then possible to formulate the actual content of the ritual or rite.

If, for example, I was asked to perform a Croning (see page 124), I would first ask what the initiate wanted from the ritual and why they wanted one. In other words, it is important to determine what the individual would like to receive from the experience. Then I would ask about location, timing, and the presence of guests. It is also helpful to know in advance what kind of ritual the initiate would prefer (long or short, ceremonial, happy, deep and meaningful, outside or inside, at a special location, and so on). After I obtain the specifications, I would plan the content of the ritual or rite and write it accordingly. You can be very specific or less so, depending upon your feelings. Croning, for example, falls under the domain of the Winter goddesses, so perhaps a significant occasion for it could be Yule. However, you or the initiate may prefer another time of year and this is perfectly acceptable as well. Follow your instincts and perceptions and all will be well.

The essential beginnings of any personal ritual or rite of passage are opening the circle, honoring the Goddess and Horned God, setting the scene (which means defining the reason for the ritual), and invoking chosen energies or helpers if considered relevant (such as Cerridwen for Croning). This is followed by a special time where the initiate is fully involved and honored appropriately. It is then important to thank the helpers, as well as the Goddess and Horned God, before closing the circle and commemorating the event further however you may wish.

In closing *The Wiccan Way* I would like
to share an ancient Celtic blessing with you:

May the blessing of the rain be on you—
the soft sweet rain
May it fall upon your spirit
so that all the flowers may spring up
and shed their sweetness on the air.

May the blessing of the great rains be on you
May they beat upon your spirit
and wash it fair and clean
and leave there many a shining pool
where the blue of heaven shines,
................and sometimes a star ✶

Open your heart and let the blessings flow.
Blessed Be!

CHILD BLESSINGS

S ince the most ancient of days, pagans have called for the presence of the three Fates at the birth of each child. The Fates are very likely connected to the Triple Goddess and her three aspects of maiden, mother, and crone as well as to the three lunar phases of waxing, waning, and full. They are known in many traditions. As the Norns in Norse mythology, the Moirae from Greece, and the Wyrd Sisters (the word Wyrd originating from the Saxon word for "fate").

The three Nordic fates—the Norns

Urdh, whose symbol is the spinning wheel, is the "spinner" or creator of a new life; color white.

Verdhandi, whose symbol is the weaving loom, is the "weaver" or recorder of each mortal's life; color red.

Skuld, whose symbol is the crescent knife, is the cutter of life threads that releases into death; color black.

A child blessing ritual

There is no altar in this ritual. You will need a bowl to contain the bottled spring water; a piece of thin red cord; and a 12-inch (30-cm) square of black cotton cloth. You will also need some sweet offerings for Skuld (see step 5). The ritual is written for a "mother" and "father," but you can either ask for the assistance of a friend or adapt this if you are single.

❶ Lay the four Wiccan tools placed in their appropriate directions on the floor or ground. Place the child comfortably in the center.

❷ The father picks up the child and takes it to each of the four directions, saying at each one, "Guardians, I bring you a new life. I ask that you

stand in protection over him/her—[or alternatively state the child's name]—*and guide him/her well from this day on."*

❸ The mother picks up the child, and the father picks up the bowl of water to assist. The mother faces North and says, "Urdh, (oorda) Earthen Mother, I ask that you bless this child with your ageless Wisdom." The mother takes some water and draws a diamond with an equal-armed cross in its center on the child's forehead.

4 The mother turns South-East and says, *"Verdhandi, she who shall weave the threads of this life together, I ask that you craft a fair and halesome cloth, with many splendid colors twined."* The father gently attaches the red cord around the babe's left wrist. (Remove the cord after the ritual and keep it safe.)

5 The mother turns to face South-West. She places the 12-inch (30-cm) square black cotton cloth gently over the baby's head and says: *"Skuld, she who stands at the threshold of each mortal soul's departing. May you grant this child a full and fruitful life before you decree the tapestry complete."* Lift the cloth away from the baby and bundle unwrapped sweets, cakes, and fragrant gifts into it to appease Lady Skuld. (The bundle should be buried after the ritual.)

6 Both parents stand together and say:

"Lady and Lord, who gave us the precious gift of this young life, in you we entrust her/his guardianship. May your blessings pour into [state name] *and keep her/him safe from all harm. So mote it be."* Kiss the child and each other, and then celebrate the occasion as you wish.

Wiccan gifts for a newborn

You can choose any of the options below to give as a gift to a newborn child.

1. *Plant a pear tree for a girl or an apple tree for a boy if you are the parents, or give the appropriate tree as a gift.*

2. *Gather sacred water from a holy spring in a blue glass bottle to be used for the blessing of the baby.*

3. *Give a silver coin that has lain beneath the light of the first waxing to full moon after the child's birth, which will help to bring the babe prosperity and abundance.*

4. *Make a posy of flowers and/or herbs associated with love to bring love to the child's life and future.*

5. *Make a protective amulet of dried juniper berries strung on red embroidery thread, with three bells (available from craft shops) attached along its length to hang out of reach above the cradle, which will protect the child's soul as it sleeps!*

6. *Make a magical wand out of ash wood marked with the runic symbols of the child's name (see pages 94–95).*

SIGNIFICANT OCCASIONS

I n today's society, we can mark significant occasions (such as birthdays, graduations, weddings, or wakes) with parties, religious ceremonies, or certificates. Very few of us, however, still honor such occasions as the passage from child to teen, or the first or last menstrual blood. Nor do we pay much spiritual homage to courageous souls when they triumph over personal challenges with bravery and dedication. Wiccans do honor these significant occasions and call them rites of passage. They offer a way to acknowledge and celebrate the spirit and soul of our life's experiences.

Each of us will experience significant occasions in our lives, one of which is sure to involve "endings" and "new beginnings."

The ritual below can be utilized to mark just such a "rite of passage" from one phase to another; for as one door closes, another is waiting to open.

A rite of passage

For this ritual you will need to put on the altar items that represent what it is that you are leaving behind or have just completed (such as—in the passage from child to teen—outgrown toys, a childhood cap, and an outdated photograph). You will also need two large squares of fabric (one black and one violet) and two candles, one black and the other violet. Then choose objects that represent your new phase or what you wish to call in. These can be symbolic, such as a book and pen for calling in a new course of study, or a "stang" for a boy who is going from his childhood into his teenage years. A stang is a long-handled, forked stick (with a shape similar to a "Y") that represents the Horned God. He is the spiritual guide for all men, guardian of the natural world and the Earth, and protector of the Goddess and her creations.

You can also make this an occasion by inviting others. Your guests could bring an appropriate gift for the "new you."

❶ Lay out your altar facing North, with a black cloth and a black candle. Burn cypress essential oil (cypress being the tree of endings). Light the candle, open your Wiccan circle, and gather around the altar silently a few moments, considering the door that is about to close. Say a few words to the Goddess and the Horned God that acknowledge your life up to this point. Those present are now invited to offer verbal or symbolic contributions to your ending.

❷ Extinguish the black candle and bundle the items into the black cloth. Ring a bell. Put the bundle under the altar. Spread out your violet cloth; and place your violet candle, peppermint essential oil, and new items toward the East.

❸ Turn clockwise from North to East, ringing a bell as you go. Facing East, light the violet candle. Then declare your new intent or phase and welcome it in. This is the opportunity for giving and exchanging gifts. Call for the door to open before you by ringing a bell again.

❹ Close your circle. Your new items can be displayed on any eastern wall of your home (such as on a mantelpiece or in a special area) or left on the altar until the new door opens.

HANDFASTING

H andfasting is the pagan term for "marriage." This ritual is not legally binding. It is a joyful and meaningful ceremony that is filled with symbolism from more ancient times. Most couples pledge their hearts to each other for a year and a day, after which they choose either to deepen their vows or to part. There are three levels of commitment that couples can make: a year and a day, while love lasts, or for a lifetime.

A handfasting ceremony is best performed outdoors, weather permitting, with someone other than the couple holding and guiding ceremonial proceedings.

You will need a cauldron filled with flowers; about one yard (one meter) of thin, red cord; the rings; a sword or blade; a small cushion; a pentagram; and a chalice filled with red wine.

❶ Set up your altar to the North with the chalice on your pentagram in the center. Place the sword to one side, the cord in front of the chalice, and a small cushion for the two rings at other side of the sword. Put the flower cauldron in the center of the circle, and invite the couple to kneel together (she left, he right) at the altar as you cast the Wiccan circle.

❷ Everyone stands and moves to the East. Place one hand on each shoulder. The facilitator of the event says: "*Guardians of the East, I bring you* [state the couple's names here]. *Bear witness to their pledge and bless their union with your (truth, grace, and knowledge).*" Take them to the South and repeat the same blessings, replacing the last words with ("honor, passion, and courage"). Take them to the West and repeat as before but with ("love, compassion, and sweetness"). Take them to the North and repeat as before with ("stability, nourishment, and richness"). All return to the altar.

❸ Take up the sword/blade and give it to the man. Stand before him and say, "*Lord, take up thy sword and make thy pledge to the maid who has won your heart.*"

The man says: "*My lady, from this day on, I pledge to love you, protect you, and serve you with honor.*" He touches her left shoulder and right shoulder with it. She takes the sword, touches her forehead, and says, "*My Lord, I accept your pledge.*"

❹ Give the chalice to the woman and say: "*Lady, take up thy chalice and make thy pledge to the Lord who has won your heart.*" The woman then says: "*My Lord, from this day on, I pledge to love you, cherish you, and fill your heart with beauty.*" She touches his heart with the chalice. He takes a sip and says, "*My Lady, I accept your pledge.*"

❺ Hand the couple the rings to place on each other's fingers. You now say, "*Mighty Ones, bear witness to this union made in love and honor, for* [state length of agreed commitment here] *between* [state their names]." Take his left and her right hands, bind them loosely together with the red cord, and say: "*In the names of the Goddess and Great Horned God, I now proclaim you man and wife.*" The couple jump over the cauldron, which symbolizes fertility, opportunity, and protection of their union.

Close your circle and celebrate.

CRONING

C roning is the honoring of a woman when she has ceased menstruation or reached the menopause. It marks the end of the female's fertile cycle and the cessation of her periods. Her menstrual blood stops flowing from her body, symbolizing that the gifts of the Goddess now flow within rather than through the woman's form. Wisdom and understanding are the gifts that come with age or experience, and a croning ritual venerates these gifts. The aspiring Crone can also contribute thoughts and suggestions about her own ritual.

You will need three cords (white, red, and black), a circlet made of ivy fronds and red silk poppies for the head, a pentagram platter, and a chalice filled with elderberry wine. An ideal gift for a croning is a cauldron, or a wand made of elder wood (the tree of crones and witches).

❶ Set up your altar to the North with two altar candles (red and white) and one small black candle secured into a portable cauldron or dark bowl. Place the pentagram in the center surrounded by the cords. The circlet of poppies should be behind the pentagram or to the right, and the chalice should be to the left. Light the red and white candles, and open your circle in the usual way.

❷ Light your cauldron candle and dedicate your ritual to the Lady Cerridwen by asking the initiate to hold the lighted cauldron while you say:

"Our Lady Cerridwen, keeper of the cauldron, I bring you [state the Crone's name here], *who comes to seek admission to your Sisterhood. Her blood now flows as a river of wisdom within. Grant her, most Gracious Goddess, access to your fertile lands of wisest understanding. I ask that you bestow upon her your wisdom, grace, and ageless beauty."*

❸ With the initiate still carrying the cauldron in her right hand, pass the Crone the white cord in her left hand (see opposite). Lead her to the South-East with it and say, *"Thou hast been as the sweet Maiden."* Take back the cord. Give her the red cord, lead her to the South-West, and say, *"Thou hast been as the fertile Mother."* Take back the cord and give her the black cord. Lead the Crone to the North and say, *"Now you leave these two behind and claim your place beside our Lady Cerridwen, as an Elder in the Sisterhood of the Wise."*

Using wine from the chalice, mark the Crone's forehead with the sign of a crow's foot, one of the symbols of the Crone Goddess (see right).

❹ Place the circlet upon her head and say:

"Be blessed by the Goddess, be wise and at peace, for you are now part of a wondrous circle of knowing. Let this crown be a token of the wheel of your life thus far, and this cauldron the womb of your timeless spirit. So mote it be!"

Close your circle, dance, sing, and make merry.

DEATH RITES

All of us must leave this Earth when our time comes, giving our body to Mother Earth, while our soul returns to the Source. Death is part of life. Wiccans see death not as an ending but rather as the next stage of the soul's journey. Most witches believe in reincarnation, which is the continuation of the soul lifetime after lifetime in some form or other. Whether you believe in reincarnation or not, death is a powerful force and one that touches us all. Many people turning again to the Craft today remember being witches before. These are called blood witches, meaning "once a witch, always a witch."

Death rites honor the departed friend or loved one, and help us to grieve our loss. At the same time, we also celebrate a life and give thanks for it. The death of a loved one is very personal and so with this ritual, you can add or change any part of it to suit personal requirements or individual requests.

You will need one white candle for each living person present, a photograph and/or items from the deceased, one white rose for each attendee, the pentagram, an apple, and taped birdsong (optional). Begin late afternoon.

❶ Set up your altar facing the West—the direction of the Western Isles or "Otherworld"—with the photo, items, two black altar candles, white roses, and an apple placed on your pentagram. Cast your circle as usual.

❷ Guests gather in a circle while you stand facing West. Ring a bell nine times and say:

"*Lord and Lady, we gather here at the setting of the sun, as it goes down on the life of* [state deceased's name here], *into the world beneath the downie hills. 'Tis time for* [.........] *to cross the river to the further shore and come home to you. His/her body commended to the Earth, his/her Spirit free to fly beyond the moon. Lord and Lady we ask that you take the soul of* [.........] *into your keeping. Bless his/her crossing. Blessed be.*" Ring the bell again nine times.

❸ Give each person a white rose and offer the opportunity to share memories of their relationship or experience with the deceased. Silence is perfectly all right, too. Each person holds their rose, then after sharing they place the rose by their feet.

❹ Hand each person a white candle and play the birdsong (closely associated with the journey to the Western Isles). Light your white candle from a black altar candle. Snuff out the two black candles and light the candle of the person next to you. They, in turn, light the candle of the person next to them until all candles are lit. You say, "*The sun does set, and yet it shall rise again. What was shall be once more. And so we commend the Spirit of* [.......] *to peace.*" Place the candles in a circle on the altar. Take up the apple and ask everyone present to send their thoughts, wishes, and blessings for the departed into the apple and then say: "*Take this apple to sustain you. It is filled with our love and protection. Go well, fair Spirit, until we meet again.*" Ring the bell nine times. Bury the apple, either with the person or in a chosen spot.

❺ Close your circle and invite participants to take their roses to a river and float the petals into the sunset while saying, "*farewell for now.*"

INDEX